CW00678189

Focus Groups for the Social Science Researcher

What is a focus group? Why do we use them? When should we use them? When should we not?

Focus Groups for the Social Science Researcher provides a step-by-step guide to undertaking focus groups, whether as a stand-alone method or alongside other qualitative or quantitative methods. It recognizes the challenges that focus groups encounter and provides tips to address them.

The book highlights three unique, interrelated characteristics of focus groups. First, they are inherently social in form. Second, the data emerge organically through conversation; they are emic in nature. Finally, focus groups generate data at three levels of analysis: the individual, group, and interactive level. The book builds from these three characteristics to explain when focus groups can usefully be employed in different research designs. This is an essential text for students and researchers looking for a concise and accessible introduction to this important approach to data collection.

Jennifer Cyr is Associate Professor of Political Science and Latin American Studies at the University of Arizona. She published *The Fates of Political Parties: Institutional Crisis, Continuity, and Change in Latin America* (Cambridge University Press, 2017), and has published in several journals, including *Comparative Political Studies, Comparative Politics, PS: Political Science and Politics, Studies in Comparative International Development*, and *Sociological Methods and Research*. She is co-founder of the Southwest Workshop on Mixed Methods Research and co-editor of *Qualitative and Multi-Method Research*.

Methods for Social Inquiry

Editors

Colin Elman, Syracuse University
Diana Kapiszewski, Georgetown University
James Mahoney, Northwestern University

The Methods for Social Inquiry series comprises compact texts offering practical instructions for qualitative and multi-method research. Each book is accompanied by pedagogical data and exercises.

The books in the series offer clear, straightforward, and concrete guidance for teaching and using methods. While grounded in their relevant prescriptive logics, the books focus on the "how-to" of the methods they discuss – the practical tasks that must be undertaken to effectively employ them. The books should be useful for instruction at both the advanced undergraduate and graduate levels.

The books are tightly integrated with digital content and online enhancements through the Qualitative Data Repository (QDR). QDR is a new NSF-funded repository housing digital data used in qualitative and multi-method social inquiry. The pedagogical data (and related documentation) that accompany the books in the series will be housed in QDR.

Focus Groups for the Social Science Researcher

Jennifer Cyr
University of Arizona

CAMBRIDGE
UNIVERSITY PRESS

University Printing House, Cambridge CB2 8BS, United Kingdom

One Liberty Plaza, 20th Floor, New York, NY 10006, USA

477 Williamstown Road, Port Melbourne, VIC 3207, Australia

314–321, 3rd Floor, Plot 3, Splendor Forum, Jasola District Centre,
New Delhi – 110025, India

79 Anson Road, #06–04/06, Singapore 079906

Cambridge University Press is part of the University of Cambridge.

It furthers the University's mission by disseminating knowledge in the pursuit of education, learning, and research at the highest international levels of excellence.

www.cambridge.org
Information on this title: www.cambridge.org/9781107189164
DOI: 10.1017/9781316987124

First published 2019

Printed and bound in Great Britain by Clays Ltd, Elcograf S.p.A.

A catalogue record for this publication is available from the British Library.

Library of Congress Cataloging-in-Publication Data
Names: Cyr, Jennifer, 1978– author.
Title: Focus groups for the social science researcher / Jennifer Cyr.
Description: Cambridge, United Kingdom ; New York, NY : Cambridge University Press, 2019. | Includes bibliographical references.
Identifiers: LCCN 2018042781| ISBN 9781107189164 (hbk.) | ISBN 9781316638798 (pbk.)
Subjects: LCSH: Focus groups. | Social sciences – Research – Methodology.
Classification: LCC H61.28 .C87 2019 | DDC 300.72/3–dc23
LC record available at https://lccn.loc.gov/2018042781

ISBN 978-1-107-18916-4 Hardback
ISBN 978-1316-63879-8 Paperback

Contents

Tables

Boxes

Acknowledgements

As with most things early on in academia, my journey to writing this book began with my dissertation. I was studying what we now call party brands in Peru, Bolivia, and Venezuela. What came to mind when citizens thought about a political party? Did citizens regularly associate certain attributes to specific parties? Having spent quite a bit of time in each country, I knew that the standard approach to measuring the phenomenon—that of tying a party's brand to ideology via close-ended questions on a survey—was not quite right. For one, many parties had historically eschewed a consistent ideological position. This was especially the case in Peru.

But that didn't mean, for example, that Peruvians couldn't speak about certain parties and assign attributes to them. All you had to do was ask someone on the street about the *Partido Aprista Peruano* (PAP), a party with a storied and controversial past. They certainly had something to say! To me, those opinions mattered. But they weren't necessarily about ideology, and they couldn't easily be captured in a survey setting. I turned to focus groups so that I might replicate the many conversations I had with citizens on the ground. I wanted to understand how they talked about different parties and whether those discussions would travel across different settings.

These initial focus groups were difficult to organize—thanks, in no small part, to my own inexperience. But I learned a lot, and I had a lot of fun doing them. In the end, the payoff for all the hard work was quite high: I obtained a lot of useful information and added a new data collection method to my toolkit. I began to think about how I could utilize focus groups in pursuit of my other research interests.

I began to think, too, more systematically about focus groups: what they could give us that other data collections methods could not, how they might be used in conjunction with other methods, and what their (inevitable) weaknesses were. I also wondered why political science, as a discipline, did not utilize them as much as other disciplines. These questions inevitably turned into a research agenda in its own right. I owe a debt of gratitude to many for supporting me as I pursued it.

First, I thank my advisors, Edward Gibson, James Mahoney, and Jason Seawright, at Northwestern University. None of them blinked an eye when I proposed to undertake focus groups as a part of my dissertation work.

Since graduating, Jim and Jay have actively promoted my interest in focus groups. They encouraged my writings on the topic, gave me feedback on early drafts of articles, and included me in methods-based projects and workshops.

Many people, too, have helped me carry out focus groups in different countries. Their experience with focus groups helped shape my own. I learned a lot from each of them. Thanks, in particular, to Gerardo González, Carlos Meléndez, and Denisse Rodríguez Olivari, but also to the many other moderators, transcribers, and local experts for helping me strengthen my question protocols and interpret my findings.

Thank you, as well, to the wonderful organizers and participants of the Institute for Qualitative and Multi-Method Research (IQMR), at Syracuse University. I am especially grateful to the colleagues who read an early version of this text in the 2016 authors' workshop. I would also like to thank the wonderful women with whom I have helped create the Southwest Workshop on Mixed Methods Research: Marissa Brookes, Kendra Koivu, and Sara Niedzwiecki. My ability to write this book was shaped, in great part, by the fruitful conversations held over the past three workshops. May we continue to promote qualitative and mixed methods—and women in academia!—for years to come.

I am grateful to Colin Elman, Diana Kapiszewski, and James Mahoney for inviting me to participate in the wonderful Methods for Social Inquiry Series. Thanks, as well, to the manuscript's reviewers, to my editor, John Haslam, and to the editorial team at Cambridge that helped me through the book's final stages. Their feedback, flexibility, and patience were crucial for transforming an early draft manuscript into a finished product.

Their patience, in particular, was vital. While writing this book, I had my second child and was diagnosed with cancer. Both events provoked a significant loss of sleep and productivity. But only the first, of course, was planned. Magdalena has brought me nothing but joy. Breast cancer, by contrast, has forced me to confront a lot of unpleasantries: a loss of control over my body, a mostly failing health care system, unexpected hiccups on my road to recovery, and, of course, my own mortality.

These life events, planned and unplanned, have made surviving—forget about thriving!—in academia very difficult. I can confidently say that, were it not for a whole slew of people, these pages would never have seen the light of day. In addition to those I have already thanked, I would like to acknowledge the School of Government and Public Policy and the Center for Latin American Studies at the University of Arizona. As I learned how to mother two small children while undergoing surgery and chemotherapy, my SGPP and LAS colleagues organized food deliveries and covered every single one of my classes. They brought my kids toys, and prepared my husband and me dinner. They checked in regularly and nudged me (gently) to rest when the urge to work seemed overwhelming. I am so grateful for these friends, my Arizona community.

I am also immensely thankful for my family. My husband, our children, my beloved mom, my siblings, their kids, my in-laws: I cannot say enough about the support they have given and the happiness they have brought to my life. I am so blessed to know them—to be related to them! What a gift. I am who I am (all the good, not so much the bad) because of them.

And, finally, to my new family: the countless number of cancer fighters and survivors who largely go unnoticed in our daily lives. So many people told me of their experience with cancer once I began to share my diagnosis. As we compared cancer strains, chemotherapy drugs, and stories of recovery, it occurred to me that cancer is everywhere, and yet we speak so little about it. With my diagnosis I have become marked for life—as a cancer fighter, as a (soon-to-be, hopefully) cancer survivor, and as a person who, having survived, will always wonder if it will come back. These are terrible, existential burdens, and we need to share them more with others. And so I dedicate these pages to this large, and largely silent, family of which I am now forever a part. Without your strength and courage I might not have mustered my own strength and courage to move past the illness, resume my daily life, and finish writing this book. Thank you.

1 Introduction

What is a focus group? Why do we use them? When should we use them? When should we not? As a reader of this book, you may wish to know the answers to these questions. You are possibly considering using focus groups in a research project.

The primary objective of this book is to assist you in this process from start to finish, that is, from deciding if you should use focus groups all the way to analyzing and storing the data that are eventually generated. Along the way, the book includes examples of published works that have incorporated focus groups into their research design. It also provides practice exercises. By the book's end, you should know if, when, and how to undertake focus groups.

First, though, let us begin with a definition. When you think of focus groups, what comes to mind? Even if you have never participated in one, you can probably imagine what they are like. At the very least, you have likely seen a portrayal of one on TV or at the movies. Fictional examples abound. On *Mad Men*, the advertising company, Sterling Cooper, brings together a set of young women to discuss their daily beauty routines.[1] The HBO series, *Silicon Valley*, includes a focus group in which young adults absolutely skewer the new operating system of the so-called "Hooli Phone."[2] The character, Bertie, on the NetFlix series, *Love*, uses her skill-set as a focus moderator to snag a guy at a party.[3] Focus groups even made an appearance at the 84th Academy Awards, where (mock) footage from a 1920s focus group on *The Wizard of Oz* was released.[4] The list goes on and on, and includes examples from *The Simpsons* and *Parks and Recreation*, as well as a host of movies, such as *Spinning Boris* (2003) and *Our Brand is Crisis*, both the documentary (2005) *and* the movie (2015).

These fictional portrayals of focus groups are illuminating. For one, they make it clear what focus groups are. Focus groups bring individuals together to discuss a set of questions. These conversations typically take place around a table, and they include a moderator who guides and nurtures the discussion. The fictional focus groups also typically ask about some sort of product, such

[1] www.youtube.com/watch?v=RnOCGrNJSqc (last accessed July 24, 2018).
[2] www.youtube.com/watch?v=Sx1J3S6vUJ8&app=desktop (last accessed July 24, 2018).
[3] Season 1, Episode 4, "Party in the Hills."
[4] www.youtube.com/watch?v=eh6mCImeylE (last accessed July 24, 2018).

as beauty cream, a smartphone's operating system, a movie, or a presidential candidate. Individuals provide their honest feedback. The feedback becomes valuable data for the product's owner, who will use the information to improve the product and, hopefully, its reception when the product is finally launched.

As a consumer of these shows, I find these fictional depictions amusing. As a social scientist who uses focus groups regularly in her substantive work, I also tend to find them bemusing. This is because they typically emphasize the use of focus groups as a marketing tool. To be sure, focus groups have a long and storied role in marketing research (see the next section). But when we use focus groups to survey individual opinions on different kinds of products, we under-utilize the very unique strengths that focus groups provide the social science researcher.

Has, then, the fictional portrayal of focus groups been incorrect? Not exactly. Instead, I would argue that it has been incomplete. We typically only see one perspective on how to use focus groups: the marketing perspective. But, as this text hopes to illuminate, focus groups are remarkably versatile. They can be helpful in answering a variety of questions. In most cases, focus groups are useful precisely because they are more than just a space for acquiring multiple individual reactions to a product or question. When it comes to the value of focus groups for the social science researcher, the whole tends to be greater than the sum of its parts.

What, then, is it about focus groups that make them useful for social science researchers? Let us begin, first, with a formal definition of the method. David Morgan, a sociologist with a long history of writing about and working with focus groups, provides a useful definition. A focus group is a "research technique that collects data through group interaction on a topic determined by the researcher" (Morgan 1996, 130).

Why is this definition so helpful? First, it is simple and straightforward. Second, it stresses that focus groups are a data collection method, or an approach to gathering data on a topic. They are, in fact, a *qualitative* data collection method. Researchers use focus groups to get at the substance of what people say. This substance is more important than quantifying the data for statistical purposes. Focus groups excel in revealing *what* participants think and *why* they think as they do (Bratton and Liatto-Katundu 1994, 537).

Third, the definition reminds us that, although focus groups generate data through participant discussions, the researcher nonetheless has a role in defining the topics that are discussed. As we will see moving forward, the creation of a question protocol (Chapter 3) and its execution by the focus group moderator (Chapter 4) are key elements in determining whether the method will be successful or not.

Finally, and most importantly, the definition highlights the social and interactive nature of focus groups. In fact, focus groups are one of the few *inherently social* data collection methods that social science researchers have at their disposal. Focus groups create data from the twists and turns of the conversation as it unfolds – what we call an *emic* approach to data creation. Although focus groups are often used to survey multiple individual opinions simultaneously (see, e.g., Cyr 2016), they can and, as we will see, often *should* privilege the social nature of the world around us.

We can build off these points to come to the fundamental premise of what follows in this book: **The advantages of focus groups for the social science researcher are grounded in three interrelated characteristics of the data collection method.** First, focus groups are **social** in form. Second, the data are generated through largely **emic** processes. Finally, focus groups produce data at **three levels of analysis**: the individual, group, and interactive level. Taken together, these three characteristics give the focus group certain competitive advantages over other data collection methods. First, focus groups allow researchers to understand group processes and dynamics. Second, they are quite empowering for focus group participants. As we will see in what follows (this chapter and also Chapter 2), these two advantages allow researchers to address certain questions that may not be feasible via other data collection methods.

Before we get to this point, however, it might be useful to first understand how focus groups have historically been used. As we will see, the three characteristics that this book highlights have not always been considered the method's primary features. Instead, how they have been used has changed fairly dramatically over time.

A Brief History of Focus Groups

The Development and Early Uses of Focus Groups

Sociologists first used focus groups to examine citizen attitudes on US involvement in World War II. These scholars observed a group of individuals watch and then react to a radio morale program that the US government was testing (Merton 1987, 552–553). Following the program, the individuals were asked to share and explain their reactions to it. Focus groups emerged largely in response to the deficiencies that the sociologists identified in that follow-up, group interview. The sociologists eventually published an article (Merton and Kendall 1946) and then a book (Merton et al.1956) on how properly to use the method.

The sociologists who formalized the so-called 'focussed [*sic*] interview'[5] emphasized four key characteristics of the data collection method: (1) non-direction, or openness with respect to the structure of the interview questions; (2) specificity, or the need to elicit precise answers from participants on particular phenomena; (3) range, or the goal of generating as much data as possible; and (4) depth and personal context, or the need to extract as many self-revelatory comments as possible on the material in question (Merton and Kendall 1946, 541–545). Although developed initially by sociologists, focus groups became particularly prominent early on in the field of marketing (Fern 2001, 3; Hollander 2004). There, researchers used focus groups to understand what, if anything, was noteworthy or salient about a particular product (Calder 1977).

Two additional points bear mentioning regarding the development of focus groups as a data collection method. First, focus groups were never envisioned as a stand-alone method. Instead, focus groups were seen as either post-tests for or precursors to quantitative methods. Merton, for example, believed that focus groups should be used to interpret the results of statistical analyses. Focus groups, on their own, lacked "scientific exactitude" (Merton and Kendall 1946, 543); one could glean very little from them without further quantitative testing.

Second, although the term, "focussed interviews," would eventually give way to focus groups (Merton 1987), there was little in their original conception that involved the group dimension of the data collection method.[6] Indeed, the World War II tests upon which focus groups were based elicited *individual* reactions to the radio morale programs. Moreover, there was nothing in the method's four key characteristics that necessitated a group environment. One could achieve non-direction, specificity, range, and personal context without exploiting the conversations and interactions that constitute a focus group. Especially for marketing purposes, where the method gained early prominence, the "group" element of the focus group was secondary to the desire for (individual) reactions to stimuli (Cyr 2016).

The group dimension of the method became more salient with the use of focus groups in clinical psychology, sociology, and socio-psychology. These disciplines engaged in group analysis and therapy (clinical psychology), group dynamics and behavior (sociology), and the effect of these on the individual (socio-psychology) (Stewart et al. 2007, Chapter 1). For these disciplines, focus groups were more than just a venue for eliciting multiple individual reactions.

[5] Merton preferred the term 'focussed interview' to refer to the data collection method he formalized. Since then, the term 'focus group' has become predominant.

[6] In fact, Merton believed the data collection method could be used for interviews with groups *and also* individuals. By the 1970s, however, books on qualitative methods associated (or, in Merton's terms, "conflated") the "focussed interview" of Merton and his colleagues with the focus group (Merton 1987, 563). Any reference to focused interviews with single individuals was lost.

Instead, focus group conversations replicated the social processes that constituted social identities and knowledge (Farnsworth and Boon 2010, 610). Focus groups became a venue for observing those processes in action (Munday 2006, 95). Rather than privilege the individual, the method's *social* nature became increasingly salient.

Focus Groups in the 1990s: A Resurgence

Focus groups eventually "fell out of favor" during the 1960s and 1970s, when experimental and quantitative methods emerged in full force (Stewart et al. 2007, 6). By the early 1990s, however, a renewed interest in qualitative methods sparked a *renaissance* of sorts for focus groups (Hollander 2004, 607). In 1994 alone, focus groups appeared in over one hundred peer-reviewed articles (Liamputtong 2011). This resurgence in the use of focus groups in social science research was accompanied by a proliferation of textbooks and edited volumes that addressed focus groups exclusively (Stewart and Shamdasani 1990; Morgan 1993; 1996; Krueger and Casey 1994; Kitzinger and Barbour 1999; Bloor et al. 2001; Fern 2001) and in conjunction with other qualitative research methods (e.g., Finch and Lewis 2003).

These works highlighted the important role that focus groups played in providing insights into complex behaviors and emotions (Morgan and Krueger 1993), the exploration of shared experiences and identities (Barbour and Kitzinger 1999), and sensitive topics (Farquhar and Das 1999; Kitzinger 1994, 112; Morgan 1996; Wellings et al. 2000). For these scholars, focus groups were uniquely important because of their inherently social nature. They highlighted the "rich experiential information" generated through focus group interactions (Carey and Smith 1994, 124; see also Smithson 2000) and underscored the potentially wide range of perspectives that focused conversations uncovered (Morgan 1996, 134).

Despite this theoretical focus on the social nature of focus groups, in practice, researchers rarely capitalized on the group and interactive dimensions (Kitzinger 1994). Instead, focus groups were used largely to collect multiple individual reactions simultaneously (Carey and Smith 1994, 125), an approach that, again, had become predominant in marketing (Lezuan 2007, 130; Munday 2006). By the end of the 1990s, the marketing approach to focus groups had become the "accepted norm" in social science research (Liamputtong 2011, 12).

Focus Groups at the Turn of the Century

Since the beginning of the twenty-first century, the role of focus groups in social science research has been ambiguous. On the one hand, with technological advancements and the proliferation of internet access, the number of formats for organizing focus groups has increased. No longer limited to the face-to-face format, researchers undertake focus groups over the telephone and online (Gaiser 2008; Smith et al. 2009; Gothberg et al. 2013). The expansion of focus groups venues has made them increasingly accessible for researchers both in terms of their cost and the audience that can be reached.

Still, the use of focus groups in the social sciences, and in sociology and political science in particular, plummeted after its relative peak in the 1990s. In the two most highly ranked journals in each discipline (Gerber and Malhotra 2008), focus groups appeared in less than 1.5 percent of the articles published between 2004 and 2013.[7] A more inclusive search, in which all sociology and political science journals were included, uncovered a similar proportion of articles (Cyr 2016).

Additionally, of the articles that included focus groups, at least 50 percent of them focused on the individual, rather than the group or interactive, level of analysis. Well into the twenty-first century, in other words, researchers are still de-emphasizing some of the unique dimensions of focus groups as a data collection method. Indeed, what this brief history of focus groups has shown is that certain key characteristics of the focus group method have historically been under-exploited. In particular, researchers tend to privilege the individual level of analysis in their research. Consequently, the focus group's inherently social nature remains under-utilized. As we will see in the chapters that follow, this focus on the individual comes not only at the expense of the types of data generated within the focus group setting. It can also threaten the validity and the reliability of the data analysis.

An Agenda Moving Forward

Despite the apparent decrease, after the 1990s, in the use of focus groups in the social sciences, it is clear that interest in understanding and undertaking focus groups remains high. For one, publications on specific themes associated with the practice and ethics of focus group-based research continued to emerge well into the twenty-first century. These include: an examination of focus group interactions oriented toward the linguistics discipline (Marková 2007); the use of focus groups for approaching sensitive and/or difficult topics, especially in the area of health (Liamputtong 2011); an analysis of focus groups as one determinant of public opinion

[7] The journals included were *American Political Science Review* (APSR), *American Journal of Political Science* (AJPS), *American Sociological Review* (ASR), and *American Journal of Sociology* (AJS). Focus groups appeared in 0.47 percent of APSR articles; 0.34 percent of AJPS articles; 0.72 percent of ASR articles; and 1.42 percent of ASJ articles (Cyr 2016, 237).

(Myers 2008); and the use of focus groups in cross-cultural and developing country settings (Hennink 2007).

Moreover, my personal interactions with others at academic conferences, invited presentations, and at my home institution confirm that there is strong and widespread interest in undertaking focus groups. Scholars and students alike recognize that focus groups can be useful for addressing certain aspects of their research question. Yet, persistent doubts about *how* to use focus groups with rigor and transparency make them reluctant to use the data collection method.

The primary aim of this text is to make focus groups more accessible in practice for those who wish to use them in their work. It pursues this aim by highlighting three interrelated characteristics of focus groups – characteristics that will help us understand when and how to best take advantage of the data collection method. The next section describes each of these, setting the stage for what follows in the rest of the book.

Three Interrelated Characteristics of Focus Groups: A Basis for Their Use in the Social Sciences

The potential utility of focus groups for a variety of research agendas is well known. Their advantages are multiple. Focus groups are an efficient method for collecting qualitative data with multiple participants. They provide a safe environment for sharing ideas and perspectives on sensitive or difficult topics. Focus groups privilege spontaneity. They represent a space where personal problems can be discussed openly (Onwuegbuzie et al. 2009, 2; see also, Morgan 1988; Duggleby 2005; Barbour 2008). Certainly, these are valuable guideposts that signal when focus groups may be an appropriate data collection method. It is difficult, however, to fully comprehend when and why to use focus groups without understanding the methodological foundations that underpin this list.

On this point, this text highlights three interrelated characteristics that help distinguish focus groups methodologically from other data collection methods. These are associated with the focus group structure, process, and the types of the data generated. First, focus groups are inherently **social** in form. Second, focus groups produce data that are **emic** in nature. Third, focus groups generate data at **three levels of analysis**. Each of these attributes may not be unique to focus groups. Taken together, however, they help determine when and how focus groups can be useful for our research. Chapter 2 addresses this point in much greater detail. First, however, we must better understand what each of these characteristics entails.

The Social Form of Focus Groups

Focus group conversations are inherently *social* in their form. Participants are likely to consider the presence of others before they give their opinion. This means that what focus group participants say is subject to the same social pressures that affect individual behavior in the real world. For some, this means that individual participants cannot be treated as independent from one another.[8] It also makes focus groups uniquely capable of measuring how we gain knowledge on certain phenomena in real life.

To make sense of this, let us consider an example of how meaning can be acquired via social processes. As you know, two political parties currently dominate the party system in the United States: the Republican and Democratic parties. Both parties have a fairly solid set of partisan followers (known as Republicans and Democrats). As ample research has shown (e.g., Green et al. 2002), these partisans have acquired fairly stable group identities based on certain policy preferences. Republicans tend to favor small government and more conservative fiscal and social policy. Democrats, by contrast, tend to support a larger, more active government, particularly when it comes to distributive policy. They also espouse more progressive social policies.

These identities were forged through eminently social processes. Partisans embody certain traits in their everyday activities and conversations (Green et al. 2002, 11). Others recognize these traits across the multiple partisans they encounter. Over time, these traits become descriptive of the partisan in general, helping to produce and reinforce group identity. Consequently, individuals identify as Democrat or Republican through social processes. Party traits and stereotypes are learned via inherently social processes (Ehrlich 1973; Leyens et al. 1994).

From this example on partisan identity we can draw two conclusions. First, it is through our groups (e.g., our family, our friends, our colleagues, our

[8] On this point there is some debate. Can an individual speak freely in a group setting, such that what she says is unaffected by that group setting? Some scholars find that the social pressures operating within the focus group setting make it very difficult for individuals to speak their mind without being influenced by the group. Consequently, they conclude, we cannot treat the individual responses of participants in a focus group as independent from each other (Carey and Smith 1994; Kidd and Parshall 2000; Schindler 1992; Sim 1998). Others, however, contend that individual opinions are formed as a result of fundamentally social processes. We can, therefore, use the focus group to observe this process of individual opinion formation (Vicsek 2010, 131; see also Kitzinger 1994; 2004; Kosny 2003; Puchta and Potter 2002; Wilkinson 2006). In practice, the individual is treated as an independent unit in many studies that use focus groups (Cyr 2016). There are also certain tricks that the researcher can adopt to measure if these kinds of social pressures are at play (see Chapter 4). Finally, social desirability bias operates in multiple different data collection methods, including interviews and surveys. Given these realities, this text adopts the position that it is possible to measure the individual as an independent level of analysis within the focus group. I return to this point in greater detail later.

bowling or garden clubs, our Facebook community) that *collective* sense of the world is made; that shared meanings are negotiated; and that group identities are forged (Wilkinson 1999, 225). The Democratic party develops a set of constitutive traits – its identity – as a result of the behaviors that Democrats exhibit and the ideas that they espouse. Second, individuals develop *their own* understanding, opinions, and perspectives of the world, as well as their place in it, through social processes (Albrecht et al. 1993, 54). An individual comes to identify (or not) as a Democrat precisely because of what she has learned about Democrats through her conversations with family, friends, colleagues, etc.

Because of their social nature, focus groups replicate these processes. For one, focus groups simulate group dynamics that occur in real life. Researchers can organize focus groups around individuals who share certain traits or experiences (e.g., women, union members, domestic violence victims). These commonalities bind individuals together to form groups in the *sociological* sense, such that "the collectivities are more than simple sums of the individuals who comprise them" (Short 2006, 107). Still, the group dynamic can also develop around quite minimal criteria, such as a common shirt color or the shared experience of participating in a focus group (see, e.g., Tajfel 1970; Tajfel et al. 1971; Frank and Gilovich 1988). The social nature of focus groups allows researchers to tap into group synergy (Stewart et al. 2009, 594).

Additionally, focus groups replicate the social manner through which *individuals* form their opinions. Focus group participants develop or refine their views in reaction to what other participants say (Farnsworth and Boon 2010, 609). Consequently, practitioners must keep in mind that focus groups are an "exercise in group dynamics" (Stewart and Shamdasani 1990, 7). The social nature of the group is a factor to consider when deciding if focus groups are useful for a research project.

The social nature of the focus group means that certain topics are not appropriate for study in a focus group setting. For example, a researcher who wishes to obtain individual narratives should probably not adopt focus groups as a data collection strategy. Here, the group setting can be a distraction (Barbour 2008, 18). This is not to say that social processes did not, in some way, affect that individual narrative. Certainly they did! Still, focus groups will make it difficult to access the individual's story in an uninterrupted fashion.

In many cases, however, the inherently social nature of focus groups, and the group pressures and dynamics therein, are actually vital for understanding the research topic of interest. Consider, for example, the partisan identity example above. The construction of the Democratic identity occurs inter-subjectively, that is, as partisans engage with each other and with non-partisans. How we, as individuals, understand partisanship in the United States tends to be shaped by how partisans are discussed at our dinner table, in school, in the office, on the television, or in social media.

We can draw a similar conclusion for other concepts, including race, gender, charisma, identity, power, or legitimacy. Our understanding of these phenomena is often highly contextual and acquired via inter-subjective processes, that is, in our interactions with others. For these kinds of socially constructed concepts, focus groups are particularly useful. This is because focus groups replicate the social processes through which meaning is acquired and forged.

Finally, ample research has shown that the social dimension of focus groups can facilitate and ease the discussion of certain, more sensitive topics (see, e.g., Farquhar and Das 1999; Liamputtong 2011). For example, focus groups can be empowering for individuals who suffer from a traumatic illness, such as HIV/AIDs or breast cancer (see, e.g., O'Brien 1993b; Carey 1994). When participating in a focus group with individuals who have shared the same experience, individuals may be more likely to share their own story. Additionally, as Barbour (2008) reminds us, the extent to which a topic is taboo or sensitive will vary by individual. The group setting can assuage feelings of discomfort on the part of some individuals, because others might be willing to open the conversation and, consequently, "break" the taboo (Barbour 2008, 18).

The Emic Nature of the Data Produced

In addition to its social form, focus groups generate data that are *emic* in nature. We typically contrast emic research with etic research. These represent two different ways of studying people. Emic research entails gathering data from the perspective of the subject. The idea behind this kind of data collection is that the researcher draws from the conceptual schemes and categories that the group deems to be meaningful and appropriate (Lett 1990, 130). In other words, researchers learn about a phenomenon via the descriptions offered by a particular group or culture. Emic data privilege the *subject's* viewpoint.

Etic research, by contrast, privileges a set of theories, perspectives, or concepts previously developed within the researcher's discipline. The idea behind this data collection is to measure whether that existing theory or perspective applies to the new group or culture. Here, the *researcher's* perspective on the phenomenon in question, and her hypotheses regarding that phenomenon, are privileged (see, e.g., Krippendorf 2004; Kottak 1996).

In practice, no data are generated via a purely emic or etic approach. Researchers do not (nor should they!) adopt an emic approach to data collection without having some sense of what the existing literature says about the topic in question. Similarly, researchers rarely apply a model or theory to a new group or context without having some knowledge or sense beforehand about that group or context. Instead, data collection methods tend to privilege one approach or the other.

Focus groups privilege an emic approach to data collection. The researcher typically poses less structured questions, with the goal of letting participants speak freely about the issues raised. Data emerge from conversations that, while initiated by a question, unfold through the potentially multiple and diverse responses of the participants.[9]

To be sure, the fact that there is a question protocol implies a certain amount of researcher-imposed structure on the focus group. Nonetheless, focus group questions should be open (Merton and Kendall 1946), allowing for a participant-led conversation to organically flow, with only minimal interruption by the moderator. Participants can use their own words, their own categorizations, and their own perceived associations in answering a question (Stewart et al. 2007, 40). Overall, focus group participants enjoy a high degree of freedom to respond as they wish (Stewart et al. 2009, 590).[10] Especially in comparison with survey-based research, which tends to privilege closed-ended questions that are crafted (and therefore "imposed") by the researcher, focus groups privilege the participants' perspective.

The spontaneity of the exchanges that occur in the focus group setting, and the emic data that these exchanges produce, represent a unique advantage of focus groups (Stevens 1996, 171). They become a good choice for researchers who are embarking on a new research agenda. Focus groups are excellent for gathering data where little data currently exist (Copsey 2008). By allowing participants openly to deliberate on a set of questions, focus groups provoke hypotheses that can later be tested via other means (Prabhakar 2012, 81; see also Merton 1987). For example, Prabhakar (2012) used focus groups as an initial method for exploring how the British public viewed government spending and taxation. The longer-term research agenda centered on the design of effective tax systems. The focus groups provided an initial set of responses that could later be tested using other, large-scale methods.

Second, focus groups are useful for studying decision-making processes, including how people assess different priorities or tradeoffs (Barbour 2008). Generally speaking, focus groups allow researchers to see how people think, what factors they take into account in making a decision, and how and if these

[9] This can create some issues with comparability across focus groups. After all, the researcher cannot know how the conversation will evolve. The same question can provoke very different responses in different focus groups, because the participants will be different. As we will see moving forward, however, it is nonetheless possible to analyze data across focus groups that ask the same set of open questions.

[10] Other data collection methods that privilege emic research include unstructured individual in-depth interviews, projective methods, and ethnographies (Stewart et al. 2007, 40).

factors are resolved once the decision has been made. Given their social nature, focus groups are particularly effective at studying group norms, group meaning, and group decision-making processes (see, e.g., Bloor et al. 2001).

For example, one study examined whether targeted social policies engender a more inclusive sense of citizenship among recipients (Hunter and Sugiyama 2014). The researchers undertook eleven focus groups with recipients of one targeted social policy, Brazil's *Bolsa Família*, and asked them to consider whether that policy had a positive effect on their own feeling of inclusion in the community. The researchers learned from group discussions that *Bolsa Família* generated feelings of agency and empowerment (Hunter and Sugiyama 2014, 835). Despite acknowledging serious problems with the program, the groups ultimately (and universally) decided that it engendered a sense of inclusion.

Finally, the emic nature of focus groups allows researchers to understand how participants talk about a topic of interest (Stewart et al. 2009, 591). This can be particularly useful in a mixed-methods research design, where focus groups are used as a pre-test for developing valid survey questions (Copsey 2008; Morgan 1996; Stewart and Shamdasani 1990; see also, Fuller et al. 1993). The emic nature of focus groups allows researchers to test and refine survey question phrasing. They can also check for cross-sectional comparability. Does the phrasing of a particular question adequately tap into a topic of interest across multiple research sites? Or, alternatively, must the question be re-worded to address differences in context? Researchers in Thailand, for example, found that seemingly objective terms from a US-based survey, including "room" and "bedroom," had to be clarified before undertaking the same survey in Bangkok. Additionally, certain sayings, such as "too tired to do anything" had to be re-phrased to account for contextual differences. In Thailand, the more appropriate saying was "too tired to move" (Fuller et al. 1993, 100).

The Three Levels of Analysis of Focus Groups

One final characteristic of focus groups is related to the analysis of focus group data.[11] Specifically, focus groups can generate data at three different levels of analysis: the individual level, the group level, and the level of the interaction. This means, in practice, that one can learn a lot from focus groups! It also means that a researcher must decide *where* to focus her analytical energies after carrying out focus groups. To do this, she must understand what kind of information each level of analysis conveys. This section briefly introduces each level of analysis. Chapter 5 provides greater detail on how to analyze focus group data.

[11] This section borrows from Cyr 2016.

Researchers may wish to use focus groups as a venue for accessing multiple individual perspectives simultaneously. There is considerable debate about the value of using focus groups in this way (see, e.g., footnote 8 above; see also Vicsek 2010). It is nonetheless the case that a majority of research projects that use focus groups tends to privilege the individual level of analysis.

When researchers privilege the individual level of analysis, they are most interested in the responses that individual participants give to the questions posed. For example, DiMaggio and Garip (2011) use focus groups to understand where migrants go for help and find that "most" migrants prefer to turn to their peers rather than their families (DiMaggio and Garip 2011, 1920). The term, "most," represents a quantification of the data. The authors surveyed all individuals and found that the majority responded in one particular way.

Focus groups can be a relatively inexpensive way to "rapidly appraise" what a group of individuals think about a question or topic (Bratton and Liatto-Katundu 1994, 537). By this logic, a researcher would use focus groups because of the economy of scale they offer. Rather than undertake twenty-five to thirty in-depth interviews about a topic, which can take multiple hours and several days or weeks to complete, a researcher may instead choose to organize three focus groups. In the context of the focus group, the researcher can ask multiple individuals to provide their feedback on a particular question. This often entails literally going around the room and fielding individual responses on a particular question or concern. Consequently, in as little as six hours, the researcher can access the same number of people's views as with hours and hours of single interviews.

Individual-level responses are most easily quantified (e.g. *How many individuals agreed with Question 1? How many spoke positively about Issue A? How many spoke negatively?*). Where the responses line up with data collected via other means, focus groups can confirm or build upon that evidence. In this sense, focus groups are an additional venue to generate data. They can also provide valuable quotations that are illustrative of the general findings. Focus groups can add qualitative "meat" to the bare-"bones" data collected via quantitative methods (Posner 2005, 310). Overall, researchers who analyze data at the individual level typically use focus groups to triangulate data collected elsewhere (Cyr 2016).

It bears re-emphasizing that researchers who focus on the individual level of analysis are not as interested in leveraging the social nature of the focus group. In effect, it is difficult to isolate individual responses from the general group conversation on most questions. For example, when noting an individual response, how does a researcher know that the participant is speaking her mind rather than reacting to what someone else has said? It is difficult to know for sure that the response an individual gives in a group is similar to her response in a non-social setting. One way to get around this is to ask participants to write their responses down before voicing them. That way, researchers will have a written record of individual reactions that are uninfluenced by the group discussion.

To be sure, a unique feature of the focus group is its social setting. Therefore, rather than exclusively focus on the individual level of analysis, researchers might instead emphasize the *group* level of analysis. Much of the focus group is dedicated to participant discussion and debate on specific questions or topics. The back-and-forth that occurs allows answers to build and evolve, uncovering nuances and complexities that may be obscured by more etic-oriented data collection methods (Stewart et al. 2009, 594). By analyzing the group level of analysis, researchers can assess whether there is consensus on a particular topic, on what the topic means for the group, and/or how the topic is discussed.

In practice, this means that focus groups can be used to measure (dis)-agreement on how phenomena are interpreted or understood. For example, Gibson (2004) organized focus groups in South Africa, asking citizens to discuss racial dynamics in the country. The focus groups revealed that, though multiple races co-exist in the country, the predominant racial conflict occurred between black South Africans and all others (Gibson 2004, 205). Gibson then used the focus group findings to refine a battery of questions in a representative survey that he later administered.

Gibson focused his analysis of the focus group data on the group level. This made sense because he wished to assess how South Africans as a group understood racial dynamics. In fact, researchers who use focus groups to pre-test questions for a large-N data collection method, such as surveys or experiments, regularly analyze group dynamics (Cyr 2016; see also Fuller et al. 1993, O'Brien 1993a). When focus groups reveal consensus on a particular question, researchers can feel more confident that the survey or experimental protocol they have developed is tapping into the appropriate sentiments, beliefs, or stereotypes regarding a topic of interest. Researchers who analyze the group level of analysis tend to use focus groups as a pre-test for a more quantitative data collection instrument (Cyr 2016).

When researchers analyze the group level of analysis, they typically bypass much of the deliberation that takes place among participants to focus on the end result or conclusion of a particular conversation. Indeed, focus group conversations, as they unfold, can be quite messy. Participants may work through multiple, conflicting perspectives on a topic before arriving at consensus (Barabas 2004). The numerous interactions that constitute the discussion of one question are not, therefore, amenable for researchers who use focus groups as a pre-test.

Yet, those interactions can produce potentially surprising insights – insights that would not be accessible via other data collection methods (Morgan 1988,

12). The third and final level of analysis, that of the interaction, provides another layer of data that researchers may exploit. Focus group conversations reveal how groups formulate meaning and/or generate opinions. The process through which this occurs, however, is not necessarily linear. Consequently, focus group interactions will not easily support or contradict previously derived hypotheses. Instead, they can lead to the formulation of *new* hypotheses, which can then be tested with other methods (Merton 1987, Bratton and Liatto-Katundu 1994).

Researchers who concentrate on focus group interactions typically do so because the interactions reveal something new or unexpected. This was the case, for example, with Moore (2008). The scholar initially undertook focus groups to triangulate data collected elsewhere on familial roles and stereotypes in black, lesbian stepfamilies. The focus group revealed, however, that conventional (read: gendered) notions of motherhood exercised great influence in these non-conventional families. This unexpected insight caused the author to postulate that women in same-sex relationships seek greater responsibility for childcare and housework to construct a gendered sense of self (Moore 2008, 348). The focus group interactions provoked a new hypothesis to explore.

Researchers tend to examine focus group interactions when these reveal unexpected or unanticipated ideas. Consequently, researchers do not typically undertake focus groups with the sole purpose of analyzing their interactions. Still, as mentioned above, the emic nature of focus groups can make them an appropriate method for gathering data on that which we know very little (see, e.g., Kidd and Parshall 2000 or Prabhakar 2012). Whatever the motivation driving the use of focus groups, researchers should be attentive to the potentially new or unexpected data that interactions can derive. We will return to this point again in Chapter 5.

Overall, then, focus groups produce data at three different levels of analysis: that of the individual, the group, and the interaction. Each level of analysis conveys different kinds of information and can be used toward different ends. The individual level of analysis allows researchers to gather multiple individual opinions simultaneously. It can be useful for triangulating other data. The group level of analysis reveals consensus on topics of interest and can help a researcher pre-test questions to be integrated into a different data collection method. Focus groups interactions produce unexpected ideas or insights. They can lay the groundwork for new hypotheses.

The Use of Focus Groups in the Social Sciences

The previous section underscored three characteristics of focus groups: their social form; the emic process through which data are generated; and the three levels of analysis where data are produced. The emphasis on these traits is important. It lays the groundwork for what follows in subsequent chapters. The three traits also underscore this book's main purpose: They allow a researcher to understand if, when, and how to use focus groups in her research design. This is because, when taken together, the three traits embody certain, unique advantages of the data collection method.

First, ***focus groups allow researchers to understand group processes and dynamics***. We have seen above that the social form of the focus group replicates how social processes work in real life. Focus groups simulate the processes through which individuals and groups acquire meaning about much of the world around them. One implication of this is that researchers should use focus groups when they wish to examine how groups understand the world around them. It also means that focus groups are useful when researchers wish to observe how individuals think and act in social settings.

Second, ***focus groups are empowering for their participants***. What do I mean by this? To begin with, in focus groups, the degrees of freedom of participant responses are high (Stewart et al. 2009, 590). The social form of the focus group, as well as the emic data that are privileged, creates a setting in which participants may respond freely to the questions that are posed. They are not forced to select one potentially unsatisfactory or incomplete answer, as with close-ended questions on a survey. Instead, they choose the words they wish to use. They choose to agree or not to agree with other participants. They may even choose not to speak. It is in this sense that the focus group is empowering for the participant (Liamputtong 2011). Researchers may therefore ask questions – about, for example, sensitive topics or with marginalized groups – that might not be accessible via other data collection methods. They can also use focus groups to pursue exploratory work.

Overall, these two advantages mean that focus groups are incredibly versatile: they allow a researcher to assess a variety of different questions. Edward Fern, who has written extensively on the use of focus groups in marketing, underscores this point (2001). He finds that focus groups help undertake myriad different tasks. They help with the exploratory tasks of creation, discovery, and identification. They unveil motivations, biases, prejudices, and predilections. They also reveal information about life experience, attitudes, intention, language, and strategy (Fern 2001, Chapter 1). Notably, Fern focuses on the use of focus groups in marketing. He therefore focuses largely on how the method draws out this information at the *individual* level. We can, however, extract equally rich data at the group and interactive levels of analysis – a point that we already made above.

Once we understand that focus groups entail these three characteristics, we see that the value of focus groups for data collection is potentially very high for the social science researcher. The rest of this book is dedicated to demonstrating this point. Along the way, it will teach the researcher if, when, and how to use focus groups in a social science research design. Let us glance quickly at the journey that awaits us.

A Road Map of What Follows

The chapters that follow are designed to walk the researcher through the multiple steps involved in undertaking focus groups. They begin by first helping the researcher to assess if focus groups will be a useful addition to her research design. Specifically, Chapter 2 explains when and why to use focus groups. It provides an extensive, if not exhaustive, list of the kinds of questions that focus groups can answer and then explains how focus groups can be used as a stand-alone method, in conjunction with other qualitative methods, and in conjunction with quantitative methods. It also identifies certain tradeoffs implied with adopting the data collection method.

Chapter 3 then helps the researcher prepare for undertaking focus groups. It spells out the logistics that should be considered, helps the researcher develop an effective question protocol, provides guidelines for training the moderator, and addresses certain challenges that can arise in non-native settings and when considering more sensitive research topics. Chapter 4 addresses how actually to carry out focus groups once the logistics and question protocol are in place. It stresses the importance of the moderator in undertaking successful focus groups. It explains the different roles a researcher can have while focus groups are underway. Finally, it tackles certain challenges that can affect focus group interactions, including how to avoid group think and/or manage overly timid or overly aggressive participants.

Chapter 5 provides guidelines on how to analyze the data generated in focus groups. Rather than offer one particular method of analysis, it focuses instead on the factors to keep in mind as you analyze the content of your data. It also briefly explains how to undertake classic content analysis – by far the most common approach to analyzing focus group data. It then reiterates that focus groups can produce data at three different levels of analysis and details when and why each level of analysis should be analyzed. Finally, this chapter provides guidelines for presenting your findings. Chapter 6 provides a brief conclusion.

In addition to providing a step-by-step guide to undertaking focus groups, Chapters 2, 3, 4, and 5 end with a series of exercises. These exercises should help the researcher put into practice some of the learning milestones of each chapter. They are designed to facilitate comprehension and further enhance the experience of planning and undertaking focus groups.

2 When to Use Focus Groups

In Chapter 1, we learned about three characteristics of focus groups that, when taken together, give the method certain unique advantages. Focus groups are social in form. They create data through emic processes. Data can be generated at three different levels of analysis: the individual, the group, and interactive levels.

In practice, these traits help make focus groups uniquely suited for understanding group processes and dynamics. They can also enable a researcher to understand how individuals think or act in social settings. Either way, it is important to underscore that the social setting of the focus group cannot be set aside. Even when researchers analyze data at the individual level, they must keep in mind that individual responses are likely shaped by the group environment. Individuals will be influenced by the responses of others; they will also be influenced by the simple fact of speaking in front of a group.

The three characteristics of focus groups also have the effect of empowering their participants. The researcher puts forth a set of questions for participants to consider. Ultimately, however, the participants decide what they want to address and if they wish to take the conversation in a different direction. Having acknowledged specific focus group characteristics and certain advantages that these bring, we can discern when focus groups are useful for the researcher. Specifically, we can identify the kinds of questions that focus groups can help answer. We can also, I should note, detect when focus groups may *not* be appropriate.

This chapter is dedicated to these tasks. It first considers the kinds of questions that focus groups can effectively address. It then offers multiple alternatives for how to address them: either as a stand-alone method, in conjunction with other qualitative methods; or in conjunction with quantitative methods. Finally, the chapter highlights certain challenges that can arise when using focus groups. These challenges are important to keep in mind, because they allow us to identify situations where focus groups would not be appropriate. By the end of the chapter, the researcher should have the tools to decide if and when to use focus groups in their research design.

Research Topics That Are Focus Group Friendly

It is not particularly instructive for you, nor feasible for me, to produce an exhaustive list of questions that focus groups can effectively address. It is possible, however, to provide an expansive list – one that can provide the researcher with a good foundation for assessing whether her specific topic could be addressed using focus groups. It may not surprise the reader to know that this list is based on what we have already learned thus far about the data collection method. And, in fact, much of what we will discuss more formally below was first mentioned in Chapter 1.

First and foremost, the list of questions that follows takes into account the two focus group advantages that we have highlighted: focus groups are suited for understanding group dynamics and processes, and they can be empowering for their participants. It also takes into account the three focus group characteristics that help define those advantages. What follows, therefore, is a list of six different types of questions that focus groups can help to address. Again, while this is not an exhaustive list, it should serve as a blueprint for the kinds of questions that are amenable to focus group-based work.

Table 2.1 provides this list. It explains that focus groups are useful for: measuring socially constructed phenomena; understanding how groups think, come to decisions, and/or process information; understanding how individuals think and act within social settings; facilitating conversations on difficult or sensitive topics and/or with vulnerable groups; contextualizing concepts; and exploring a new topic of interest. Let us examine each topic in turn.

Measuring Socially Constructed Phenomena

First things first: What is a socially constructed phenomenon? We saw in Chapter 1 that partisan identities emerge through social processes. That is,

Table 2.1 Focus Groups Can Be a Useful Data Collection Method If . . .

A phenomenon under investigation is socially constructed;
The researcher wishes to understand group processes;
The researcher wants to know how individuals think and act in social settings;
The research topic is sensitive or taboo in and/or is associated with vulnerable groups;
The researcher needs to ensure that concepts are properly contextualized both within and across research settings;
Little is known about the topic of interest.

we learn what it means to be, for example, a Democrat by observing how other Democrats speak and present themselves to the world. When individuals feel affinities with the beliefs and/or actions of Democrats with whom they interact or observe, they may choose to identify as Democrat. Partisan identity, like all group identities, is forged through social processes. Its meaning is, like many phenomena or concepts, socially constructed (see, e.g., Abdelal et al. 2009).

Socially constructed phenomena are those things that we learn about or understand thanks to our interactions with others. They are concepts created by humans and, often, serve to impose some sort of order on our social world (Yanow 2015, vii). How do we, as individuals, think about race, gender, or culture? What about power? Corruption? These are all examples of socially constructed phenomena. We know this for (at least) two reasons. First, their meaning is highly contextualized. What is perceived as an act of corruption in the United States differs from one in China or Saudi Arabia (see, e.g., Andersson and Heywood 2009, 749–750; Chadda 2004; Brown and Cloke 2004). Second, their meaning can change over time (Yanow 2015, vii). What it means to be a Republican can evolve as different candidates emerge to represent the party in national or subnational positions. President Donald Trump, a Republican, is different from, say, Ronald Reagan or John McCain in terms of his rhetoric and governing style. If more and more "Donald Trumps" emerge to represent the Republican party, our understanding of what a Republican is, in general, might change.

Because socially constructed phenomena are highly contextual and variable in their meaning, it makes sense to study them with a data collection method that can capture context and nuance. Focus groups are eminently suited for this task. Participants are allowed to speak freely about the topic in question. The conversation may reveal disagreement about a concept's meaning, contradictions over that meaning, and whether, ultimately, consensus can be forged. Socially constructed phenomena are complex by nature; focus groups allow the researcher to capture that complexity. They also tend to require high-effort cognitive thought (Chaiken 1980; Krosnick 1991; Tourangeau 1984). Socially constructed phenomena are not easy concepts to grasp. Because of this, individuals tend to look for easy shortcuts (called *satisficing*) when dealing with difficult ideas on their own (Krosnick 1991; Krosnick et al. 1996). The social form of focus groups allows multiple individuals to share the burden of working through complicated ideas. Consequently, they can be more suitable than one-on-one interviews or surveys for addressing these kinds of concepts.

Understanding Group Processes

It perhaps comes as no surprise that focus groups – a group-based data collection method – are highly effective at studying group processes, including how groups think, process information, come to decisions, prioritize, and construct meaning. Focus groups are useful for studying groups who share a common identity or shared norms and goals (Merton 1987, 555). We can think here of Paluck and Green (2009), who undertook focus groups with genocide survivors, the Twa people (a Pygmy minority), prisoners in Rwanda, and members of eight different communities. In each set of focus groups, the participants shared a common identity: they had survived the genocide, belonged to an ethnic group or community, or were prisoners. The researchers wanted to see if each group responded differently to a radio program that challenged norms of deference and legitimized dissent. The groups themselves, in other words, were the subjects of study. Focus groups were one vehicle through which the researchers could access each group.

Focus groups can also consist of more heterogeneous groups. In my work on political parties in Peru, Bolivia, and Venezuela, I measure whether citizens attribute certain traits or ideas to electorally weak parties (Cyr 2017b). I hypothesize that parties that retain a broadly recognized identity or "brand" (Lupu 2013) are more likely to survive a period of poor electoral performance than those that do not. I undertook four to five focus groups in each country and asked participants to discuss each electorally weak party. The only requirement for participation was that the individuals be of voting age for the election when the parties were voted out of national government. These were extremely heterogeneous groups. My goal was not to get a sample of any particular sector of society. Instead, I wanted to show that everyday citizens could (or could not) speak meaningfully about the parties in question. Where this occurred across multiple groups, then I had evidence of a persistent party brand.

Overall, when researchers wish to understand group dynamics and processes, a focus group is an appropriate data collection method to use.

Understanding How Individuals Act in Social Settings

Individuals tend to act differently in a group than they do on their own. We can thank longstanding social science research for this finding (see, e.g., Allport 1920; 1924). Sometimes, a researcher may want to exploit the effect of the group dynamic on how individuals act, think, or speak. In this situation, the researcher privileges the individual as the unit of interest in the focus group, but she is actively engaging with its social form.

Let us return to the example of Paluck and Green (2009) to understand how this can work in practice. The researchers wanted to see if community members in post-genocide Rwanda were more willing to express dissent in private versus public settings. To test for this, they compared the levels of dissent expressed by individuals in one-on-one interviews versus in focus groups. They found that certain subsets of individuals were more likely to express dissent in private. Here, the researchers exploited the social setting of the focus group to measure individual behavior. Theirs is a prime example of using focus groups to understand how individuals act in social settings.

Facilitating Conversations on Sensitive Topics or with Vulnerable Groups

Focus groups represent a space where individuals with similar backgrounds or experiences can share and communicate with each other. While this can allow a researcher to broach any number of topics particular to a specific group or collectivity, focus groups become particularly useful when discussing a sensitive or difficult topic or when working with vulnerable groups.[1] By *sensitive* topic we mean any topic that might be "intimate, discreditable or incriminating" in nature (Renzetti and Lee 1993, ix, as taken from Liamputtong 2011, 108). By *vulnerable* groups, I refer to those that are potentially subject to discrimination, including (but not limited to) children, the elderly, ethnic minorities, immigrants, the homeless, and the LGBTQ community (see Liamputtong 2011, 109).

Why are focus groups especially useful when undertaking research on sensitive topics or with vulnerable groups? Again, the social setting of the focus group is key. Individuals may be reluctant to discuss sensitive topics, such as a traumatic event that they may have experienced, in a one-on-one interview with a researcher. When an individual knows that she is in a focus group with others like her, however, some of the pressures or discomfort associated with the topic can be shared and, therefore, diluted. In this sense, focus groups are a "forum for mutual support" (Kroll et al. 2007, 697). Liamputtong (2011) helpfully makes this point:

> Focus groups create layers of communication and, therefore, provide respondents with a safe environment where they can articulate their experiences, opinions and beliefs in the company of people who share similar experiences and hold similar beliefs (p. 110).

When it comes to sensitive topics or vulnerable groups, the influence of the focus group's social setting can actually be positive for participants, allowing

[1] Liamputtong (2011) addresses these topics in great detail and provides multiple examples.

them to speak on matters that they might not otherwise be comfortable addressing (Kitzinger 1995, 111).

Contextualizing Topics

As we will see below, focus groups have regularly been used as a pre-test for large-N, and especially survey-based, research. With focus groups a researcher can: refine question phrasing; revise close-ended questions to include the full range of responses; and ensure that all dimensions of a particular topic are covered in the survey. Focus groups are useful for these tasks because of the emic process through which data are generated. A researcher can measure how individuals in a surveyed area talk about the topic of interest and therefore feel confident that the survey protocol reflects the linguistic idiosyncrasies of the research site. Focus groups, in other words, are useful for contextualization, and they help a researcher achieve greater measurement validity in their survey protocol (Cyr 2017b; see also Morgan 1997).

For example, a group of sociologists wanted to understand how racial attitudes affected the neighborhood preferences of white and African American families in the United States (Krysan et al. 2009). They conducted an experiment in which hundreds of individuals in Chicago and Detroit were randomly assigned to watch one of several videos that showed one neighborhood but varied the racial and class composition of its residents. To ensure that the videos conveyed proper racial and class cues, the researchers first pre-tested the videos in focus groups. Once the focus groups confirmed the intended cues, the researchers were more confident that their videos accurately portrayed race and class in the two populations (Chicago and Detroit) of interest (Krysan et al. 2009, 537–538).

This example demonstrates the utility of focus groups for ensuring that survey and/or experimental protocols are properly contextualized for their intended audience. If the focus groups participants had not interpreted the videos properly, then the data gleaned would have instructed researchers on how to improve the video's content so that it validly conveyed race and class. Additionally, the focus groups in Detroit might have interpreted the videos differently from those in Chicago. In this case, the focus groups would have allowed the researchers to ensure cross-sectional comparability, and one or both videos would have been revised accordingly. Focus groups can help researchers contextualize both within and across research sites.

Although this example has shown that focus groups can be useful as a pre-test for larger-N studies, it is important to keep in mind that the context they provide can be useful in other ways. Focus groups can be used to contextualize or ground unexpected findings from a larger survey or experiment. In other words, they can be a useful follow-up or *post*-test (Merton and Kendall 1946). Focus groups can also provide useful context prior to undertaking qualitative fieldwork. They can, for example, introduce a researcher to the idiosyncrasies and dynamics of a new field site, providing useful tips on how to undertake subsequent participant observation and/or in-depth, individual interviews (Morgan 1997, 23–24).

Exploring a New Topic of Interest

Finally, focus groups can be useful for researchers embarking on a new research agenda, especially when little is known about it (Kidd and Parshall 2000). This is because the researcher can rely upon focus group participants to do the heavy lifting with respect to revealing what might be important or salient about a particular research question. Focus groups are empowering for participants precisely because they have control of what is said. In this case, researchers can use that empowerment in their favor: In letting participants take the reins, researchers can pinpoint or isolate what might be noteworthy about a new topic of interest.

We see this happening in a project on youth drug use. Although the authors were not new to this research agenda, they were new to focus groups. They decided to organize a focus group of adolescent LSD users to see, among other things, if any new information would be produced (Agar and MacDonald 1995). Although skeptical that focus groups could generate quality data (they intuited that "a few hours with a few groups guarantees only that the 'quality' in 'qualitative' will go the way of fast food" [!]), the researchers discovered something new in the focus group (p. 78) – namely, that many teenagers used the over-the-counter drug, Robitussin, as a substitute for LSD. This new information emerged thanks to group interactions – one characteristic of focus groups that makes them "shine" (Agar and MacDonald 1995, 80). The authors concluded that group interactions allowed for insights that might not (and, in their case, had not) emerge via other qualitative methods, such as interviews and ethnography. It is for this reason that researchers use focus groups for idea or hypothesis generation (Fern 1982).

One final note about the focus group that Agar and MacDonald (1995) organized. It consisted entirely of LSD-using youths who were seeking treatment for their addiction. This was a homogenous group of kids with a common, shared experience. The researchers explicitly sought to tap into that group dynamic – something they were hard-pressed to do with other qualitative methods. Additionally, the researchers were collecting data on a vulnerable and hard-to-reach group: young, illegal drug users. In one research design, therefore, multiple topics for which focus groups are appropriate overlapped. This is not unusual, and the set of six topics addressed here should not be treated as mutually exclusive. Instead, they mutually reinforce each other and, where they overlap, make the use of focus groups even more relevant.

How to Use Focus Groups

We have identified key topics that focus groups can be useful for addressing. We know, in other words, when to use focus groups. We must also consider *how* to use focus groups within a research design. On this point, there are two initial alternatives. A researcher may use focus groups as a stand-alone method. She may also use them in conjunction with other data collection methods. Should a researcher wish to design a mixed (i.e., multiple) methods research project, she will then have to decide how to use focus groups with other qualitative or quantitative methods.

To be sure, it is not feasible to explain how to use focus groups in every potential mixed-methods combination. Instead, the following pages help the researcher understand the advantages that focus groups can provide vis-à-vis other qualitative methods and in concert with quantitative methods. It also spends some time considering two different approaches to mixing methods in general: triangulation and integration. By the end of the section, a researcher should know how her particular project might effectively include focus groups.

Before we examine in detail the multiple approaches to using focus groups in a research design, it is useful first to consider how work has used focus groups. What we see is that a large majority of publications use focus groups in combination with other types of methods and most typically with in-depth interviews or as pre-tests to surveys. The use of focus groups as survey pre-tests has a long trajectory in the social sciences (Copsey 2008; Morgan 1996; Stewart and Shamdasani 1990). This was true in the 1990s (Morgan 1996, 133). It is also true in the early twenty-first century (Cyr 2016).

Indeed, in their original formulation of focus groups as a data collection method, Merton and Kendall (1946) saw them as supplementing, not supplanting, quantitative methods. They highlighted the role focus groups played in revealing the mechanisms behind the correlations that statistical methods uncovered (p. 543). Still, focus groups can also be used – and, certainly, they *have* been used – as a stand-alone method in the social sciences. In all, the most important thing to keep in mind is that focus groups, like all data collection methods, should be used in ways that are consistent with the objectives and purpose of the research project. This can mean using them as a stand-alone method, as we will consider immediately below. It can also mean, however, using them in conjunction with other methods.

Focus Groups on Their Own

Although less common in practice, focus groups can be used as a stand-alone data collection method. Perhaps the most important thing to keep in mind when undertaking a study that relies exclusively on focus groups is that the results gleaned must comprise a "sufficient body of knowledge" for the research question at hand (Morgan 1997, 21). When does one attain this kind of sufficiency from focus groups? A person whose research wishes to understand the particular dynamics of a specific group – and in particular, how that group sees itself and the world – can use focus groups (Morgan 1997, 20–21). They also serve as a stand-alone method when the experiences and perspectives sought out by the researcher are only accessible via group interaction (Liamputtong 2011, 88).

For example, Kitzinger (1994) used multiple focus groups to examine the effect of media messages about AIDS and, specifically, how each group reacted to the messages and why they reacted as they did. Focus groups were the preferred data collection method, because the researcher wanted to explore the "social context of public understanding" (Kitzinger 1994, 104). In this example, the focus group was uniquely suited for addressing the research question at hand, since the method is inherently social.

Finally, focus groups are often used in the early stages of a broader research agenda. They are useful, in other words, for undertaking an exploration of a topic about which you (the researcher) and your field know very little. For example, Prabhakar (2012) uses focus groups as a first step toward understanding public attitudes about taxation in the United Kingdom. He finds that those attitudes changed as a function of whether tax policies were viewed separately or as a group. A next phase of his project, he concludes, would use surveys to see if these findings are broadly representative (Prabhakar 2012, 87).

When used for exploratory purposes, two additional points on focus groups as a stand-alone method bear mentioning. First, as evidenced by Prabhakar (2012), this kind of exploratory work is publishable! Second, it typically represents the first of what will probably be multiple phases of a research project. In that sense, while focus groups are, strictly speaking, a self-contained method when it comes to exploratory work, their use is often oriented toward a larger project incorporating multiple methods.

Focus Groups in Conjunction with Other Methods

It is much more common to use focus groups in conjunction with other data collection methods. A meta-analysis of the use of focus groups between 2005 and 2014 in articles published in the top two political science and the top two sociology journals revealed that *every single one* utilized focus groups with other methods (Cyr 2016). *How* focus groups were used, however, varied. Some articles used them with qualitative methods and others with quantitative methods. Additionally, certain articles adopted a triangulatory, while others adopted an integrative, approach to mixing the methods. These approaches are quite different in practice, and so before we consider how to use focus groups in conjunction with other methods, let us first differentiate between the two approaches to mixed-methods work.

Triangulation Versus Integration

When a researcher engages in triangulation, she uses additional methods to cross-verify results gleaned from other methods. She compares evidence across multiple data collection methods. When more than one method provides affirmative evidence of an inference, a researcher can be more confident that the inference is "true" (see, e.g., Denzin 2006).

Triangulation is a very common approach to mixed-methods work. Still, there are certain downsides to adopting triangulation. For one, different types of data collection create different types of data. Because of this, even though one might use two or three methods to explore a particular research question, the findings from each are not necessarily comparable. Let us take, for example, a project that uses a survey as its primary data collection method and then organizes focus groups as a way to cross-verify the survey findings. This is a common approach to mixing focus groups with survey-based research (see, e.g., Posner 2005; Garvía 2007). But what kind of data would a focus group have to generate to confirm survey-based work? Surveys collect individual attitudes and opinions on a variety of topics. The survey is administered in an asocial setting, and so we can reasonably conclude that those responses are not influenced by others (except perhaps the surveyor).

We have already learned, however, that focus groups produce individual-level data that *are* influenced by the group dynamic. Are these socially influenced data comparable with the data collected via an asocial survey? At the very least, the comparison requires justification. Additionally, what does a researcher do if, upon cross-verification, the results of a particular project do not hold? Which method does the researcher discard? There are no easy answers to these questions (see, e.g., Seawright 2016).

With triangulation, a researcher uses one data collection method to confirm an inference generated by another (see, e.g., Paluck 2010). An *integrative* approach to mixed methods, by contrast, uses multiple data collection methods to actually build the causal inference. Implicit to this approach is the recognition that all data collection methods have their weaknesses (see the next section for a discussion of the weaknesses of focus groups). When a researcher integrates mixed methods, she is using the strengths of one data collection method to offset the weaknesses and/or unaddressed assumptions of others (Seawright 2016). The resulting causal inference, therefore, produces greater confidence.

For example, Paluck and Green (2009) adopt an integrative mixed method approach. They combine focus groups and interviews to test if individuals practice in public what they articulate in private in a post-genocide setting (Paluck and Green 2009, 629). Interviews registered individual's private views. Focus groups captured how those same individuals might act in a public forum. The researchers combined the methods to test the hypothesis regarding individual attitudes versus behaviors in a post-genocide setting. Notably, they utilize a particular strength of focus groups – their social form – to help build the inference.

This text recognizes that triangulation is quite common. Still, it finds it more useful to think about mixing methods in a way that brings out each method's strengths while minimizing its weaknesses. Because of this, it adopts an integrative approach to mixed-methods work. In what follows, it underscores the strengths of focus groups vis-à-vis other qualitative methods and in relation to quantitative methods.

With other qualitative methods. Focus groups can be used with other qualitative methods. Most typically, they are combined with individual interviews, where, among other things, researchers can explore how individuals speak about concepts differently in a private versus public setting (see, e.g., Paluck and Green 2009). Focus groups also allow a researcher to examine multiple ways of communicating about a subject, including via jokes, debates, and/or arguments – communicative devices that are unlikely to be utilized in an interview setting.

Focus groups can be organized either before or after interviews. Prior to interviews, focus groups allow researchers initially to pursue reactions to a series of questions. These exploratory focus groups will reveal the range of thoughts that future (individual) informants might reveal (Morgan 1997, 22). They might also help a researcher refine a question protocol, to ensure that future (individual) respondents will interpret the question similarly. Alternatively, exploratory focus groups can help a researcher define future sites for interviews. In this case, the researcher might use focus groups to choose the best location, for comparative purposes, for undertaking a second round of interviews (Morgan 1997, 22).

Overall, focus groups tend to provide greater breadth and range on a set of topics whereas interviews provide greater depth on those topics (Hesse-Biber and Leavy 2010). The data generated, in other words, are different but nonetheless complementary. Taken together, the two qualitative methods can help a researcher gain a more complete understanding of the research question at hand (Lambert and Loiselle 2008, 230).

Focus groups can also be used in conjunction with ethnography (Agar and MacDonald 1995). In this case, ethnographic research can provide the vital background information and context necessary to properly interpret focus group-generated data. Here, ethnography provides "broader frames of interpretation" (Agar and MacDonald 1995, 78). Focus groups might also precede ethnographic work. As with interviews, undertaking exploratory focus groups in potential sites (e.g., a neighborhood, a city) can help a researcher elect a future location for ethnographic work (Morgan 1997, 24).

Ethnographic work provides extended exposure to a particular place or group. Still, researchers must relinquish any control over what they observe. Focus groups, alternatively, allow a researcher to impose at least some structure to the observed conversations and interactions. Consequently, focus groups can provide specific feedback on questions or topics that may not emerge in the more natural, observational setting.

With quantitative methods. Scholars are spending increasing time considering the merits (e.g., Tarrow 1995; Lieberman 2005; Paluck 2010; Humphreys and Jacobs 2015; Seawright 2016) and potential pitfalls (e.g., Ahmed and Sil 2012; Goertz and Mahoney 2012; Chatterjee 2013) of combining qualitative and quantitative methods in a single research design. Undoubtedly, however, this kind of mixed-methods work has increased in recent years, leading to a "boom" in designs that combine qualitative and quantitative data collection strategies (Seawright 2016, 2–4). Focus groups have often been proffered as a method that can be suitably combined with quantitative, and especially survey work (Barbour 2008; Kitzinger 2005; Morgan 1996; O'Brien 1993a). This is especially the case when it comes to addressing measurement concerns in large-N work and identifying and explaining the mechanisms that underpin causal relationships.

For example, focus group researchers have long asserted that focus groups can help improve the quality of the questions used in survey-based or experimental work (O'Brien 1993a; Fuller et al. 1993; Morgan 1993; 1996; Wilkinson

1999; Kitzinger 1995; Hesse-Biber and Leavy 2010; Liamputtong 2011). On the one hand, focus group conversations can uncover or confirm the proper phrasing or terminology that informs question protocols (see, e.g., O'Brien 1993a). They can also produce vignettes and/or anecdotal material for use in questionnaires (Kitzinger 2005, 59). In some cases, focus groups are used to ensure that an "exhaustive" list of (close-ended) responses are developed for a given question (Barbour 2008, 17).

Focus groups are particularly useful in large-N studies addressing more complex or highly contextual topics, such as race, identity, corruption, power, or legitimacy. Focus groups allow participants to share the hard work involved with discussing these complicated topics. They also, importantly, replicate the process through which we come to understand what these concepts mean in real life (Farnsworth and Boon 2010, 610). What is power? When is something legitimate? What counts as an act of corruption? As we saw in Chapter 1, we tend to acquire answers to these questions via social processes, that is, through conversations with our different informal social networks. Focus groups are an appropriate venue for devising questions or vignettes around complicated, contextual concepts, because they reproduce the social setting through which we gain meaning to begin with (Cyr 2017b). Once the focus group data are collected, researchers can use the information to devise more accurate, contextually sensitive survey questions.

In each of these cases, focus groups are conducted prior to large-N studies. They are **pre-tests** for those large-scale studies. Pre-tests are preliminary tests developed to ensure that a survey or experimental protocol works as it is supposed to. Imagine undertaking a survey with 1,000 participants and discovering, *after* the survey is administered, that a question has been poorly worded and therefore seriously misinterpreted by the population of interest. That would create serious problems for the researcher! To avoid this kind of setback, a researcher can organize a set of focus groups to ensure that the survey or experimental protocol uses the appropriate language for a particular research site (or, in cross-national studies, *across* research sites). Focus groups, in other words, help to improve the measurement validity of the large-N instrument. An instrument has measurement validity if the indicators therein meaningfully reflect the concept(s) a researcher seeks to measure (Adcock and Collier 2001, 529). When measurements are not valid, then the instrument will suffer from measurement error. Consequently, any conclusions drawn from such an instrument will be biased (Seawright 2016, 33).

Focus groups can also be used to help identify the causal mechanism underpinning a relationship identified through statistical or experimental analysis (Kitzinger 2005, Paluck 2010). Indeed, focus groups were originally utilized to achieve this objective, Merton and his colleagues used group interviews to receive additional feedback on individual, on-demand responses to a radio program. The focus groups enabled Merton to interpret the quantitative findings (Merton 1987). More recent work on field experiments suggests something similar (Paluck 2010). The logic behind this use of focus groups (and, certainly, other qualitative methods) is straightforward: Whereas quantitative and experimental work can produce a number that indicates the strength of the association between a purported cause and an effect, they cannot explain *why* this association occurs.

In effect, surveys provide largely descriptive data about individuals and groups (see, e.g., Seawright 2016). For example, they can tell us how many Americans support the Democratic versus the Republican party. Experiments can isolate causal effects. They can tell us, in other words, whether Congolese citizens are more or less likely to donate bags of salt to perceived antagonistic groups in society after being exposed to a talk show about conflict resolution (Paluck 2010, 62–63). Neither method, however, can tell us *why* US citizens identify as they do or *why* different Congolese people chose to give more or less salt. Focus groups can be conducted after a survey or experiment takes place, allowing researchers to investigate why certain associations were discovered. Here, focus groups are an appropriate method for identifying causal pathways (Seawright 2016).

Thus far, we have explored ways that focus groups can meaningfully combine with a large-N study, either by strengthening the instrument used or shedding light on the associations generated through the study. In some cases, focus groups may represent the primary data collection method, and large-N methods are integrated into the research design to build off the focus group findings. For example, surveys or experiments can provide information about the *magnitude* of an effect that has been uncovered in the focus group setting. In their work on *Bolsa Família* (a conditional cash transfer program in Brazil), Hunter and Sugiyama (2014) undertake focus groups with beneficiaries of the program to investigate whether such social policies are alienating or empowering for the (means-tested and therefore potentially stigmatized) recipients. The focus groups revealed that, despite acknowledging problems with the program, *Bolsa Família* ultimately enhanced feelings of agency among beneficiaries.

The eleven focus groups they carried out showed that, against certain theoretical expectations, policy beneficiaries felt empowered as a result of their participation in *Bolsa Família*. They could not, however, reveal *how much* of an impact the policy had, especially vis-à-vis other factors that might also enhance empowerment. A follow-up survey or experiment would provide that numerical information – providing additional information about the causal impact of *Bolsa Família* on citizen agency (Seawright 2016, Chapter 8). In this extended example, focus groups are the primary data collection method. A hypothetical, follow-up large-N study could build on and add to those findings.

In all of the examples above, focus groups operate in conjunction with quantitative methods to strengthen the causal inferences gleaned. Rather than simply triangulate the findings uncovered via other data collection strategies, this section has offered different approaches to integrating (Seawright 2016) focus groups with different quantitative methods, so that the former sustain and even bolster the findings associated with the latter (and vice versa).

Challenges to Focus Group Use: Things to Avoid and Tradeoffs to Keep in Mind

Thus far, we have examined some of the advantages of focus groups; the topics that they can effectively address; and how focus groups can be used in different research designs. Our emphasis has been on the positive aspects of focus group use. No data collection method, however, is perfect. In fact, McGrath (1982) reminds us that all – yes, all! – research strategies are "bad" in that they have serious methodological limitations (p. 80, as taken from Fern 2001, 147). A fully informed researcher will be aware of the limitations associated with focus groups.

This section examines those limitations. It is useful to keep them in mind. After all, unless we know when *not* to use focus groups, we cannot fully understand when we should use them. In what follows we examine: the challenges associated with external validity and the group dynamic of focus groups; some concerns regarding the human factor necessary for executing focus groups; and additional costs associated with organizing and undertaking focus groups.

External Validity and the Group Dynamic of Focus Groups

Let us tackle two of the biggest criticisms that focus groups typically receive. The first is based on the challenges associated with the group dynamics in focus groups (see, e.g., Sim 1998). The second criticism, which is related to the first, has to do with the lack of representativeness of the data produced (Copsey 2008, 3).

We have seen that the inherently social nature of the focus group is one of its unique strengths. It is also, however, a potential source of problems. The group dynamic of focus groups is never quite the same, even across a set of focus groups in which the moderator and the questions remain unchanged. Each focus group is composed of different individuals. Therefore, the dynamics that one focus group generates may be quite distinct from those created by another. The upshot is that participants may express very different viewpoints depending upon the group in which they find themselves (Sim 1998; see also Vicsek 2010, 123).

The potential consequences of the so-called "group situation" (Vicsek 2010) on individual participants are multiple. Perhaps most importantly, it raises questions about the **external validity** of the data collection method. An externally valid method is one from which data can be generalized beyond the immediate sample. External validity allows us to draw conclusions about the population at large based on the sample of individuals from which we collected data (see, e.g., Campbell and Stanley 1963). External validity is threatened when the sampled group is not representative of the population as a whole (a problem of *population validity*). It is also susceptible to the environment in which the data collection takes place (a problem of *ecological validity*). Focus groups are vulnerable to both threats. When it comes to population validity, it is very difficult to randomly select individuals across enough focus groups to be broadly representative of a population as a whole. As we will subsequently see, however, this kind of statistical representativeness is rarely a goal of focus group-based work.

The problem of ecological validity is arguably trickier to address. One might reasonably ask if it is "normal" for individuals to sit in a circle and discuss potentially taboo or sensitive topics. The focus group setting is contrived, even if one makes efforts to make the meeting as natural as possible (see, e.g., Nickerson 2007). Scholars worry that the artificial nature of the focus group setting influences what individuals say (see, e.g., Sim 1998). Especially when the groups are composed of strangers, the dynamic of the focus group can be frustrated by a constant need to (re)define "the norms of who, in this group, speaks to whom about what" (Myers 2008, 66). Ultimately, these concerns ask us to consider two fundamental questions. First, can we really trust what individuals reveal about their attitudes, opinions, and beliefs in a focus group? Second, are those attitudes and opinions reflective of a larger group, such that what we learn from the focus group can be reasonably applied to a general theory?

Do Focus Group Participants Say What They Think?

The first question asks us to consider the possibility that, because of the group dynamic, focus group participants may feel pressured to say something that does not actually reflect their "true" opinion. This can happen because of a dynamic called group think. Group think occurs when the pressures of the focus group dynamic cause participants to feel censored or the need to conform to what others say. Group think suppresses individual opinion (Carey and Smith 1994, 124). It may also create the illusion of consensus. For a variety of reasons, participants may prefer to agree with others about a question rather than voice their opposition. A participant may be too timid to disagree, or one or two participants may dominate the conversation such that other viewpoints are silenced. Whatever the reason, the "preference toward agreement" (Vicsek 2010, 132) in focus groups can potentially bias the data generated.

Researchers can mitigate the effect of these group pressures in multiple ways. First, they can ask participants to write down their answers to a question before any discussion takes place. This tactic allows researchers to capture the participants' first reaction to the question at hand. Researchers may then compare written with spoken responses to see if they changed (an indication that group think may have occurred). Second, the researcher can ask the same question in different ways to see if the group discussion wavers or changes. The researcher may also instruct the moderator to remain vigilant of these group dynamics. She may ask the moderator to draw out responses from everyone, so that no single person dominates the conversation. She may also instruct the moderator to pay special attention to how certain questions are discussed. Do participants acquiesce or agree more quickly than one might expect? If so, the moderator may wish to dwell on those points a bit longer to see if inconsistencies or alternative opinions emerge. Finally, the researcher can compose more homogenous groups of participants. Timid participants are more likely to voice their opinion in a room of their peers (Stewart and Shamdasani 1990).

To be sure, there are tradeoffs to each of these tactics. For one, as we will discuss in Chapter 3, focus groups typically do not last longer than 1.5 to 2 hours and therefore cannot reasonably address more than ten to twelve questions. A researcher may be reluctant to spend more than one question on any particular topic. Additionally, relying on the moderator to address or mitigate certain group dynamics brings its own challenges, which we will subsequently see. Moreover, it may not be appropriate to organize focus groups comprised of homogenous groups. Finally, although researchers can compare written with spoken responses to see if group think is taking place, the extent to which this is useful will depend on the kinds of questions asked. If a researcher is interested in individual-level data, then it might be useful and appropriate to compare written with spoken responses. If she is interested in group-level data, or in the interactions that take place, then the individual written responses will not be informative.

Overall, researchers who use focus groups should accept that group dynamics are an inevitable part of the data collection method. Indeed, there are reasons to explicitly incorporate the group dynamic into one's work. As detailed in Chapter 1, focus group discussions "mimic the natural process of forming and expressing opinions" (Schutt 2011, 309). The researcher should expect, therefore, that participants "qualify" their answers and/or "identify important contingencies" as a conversation evolves (Stewart et al. 2009, 590–591). In this sense, the group pressures that imbue focus groups give the method *greater* ecological validity than those that assess opinion formation in asocial settings (Albrecht et al. 1993, 54).

Overall, the underlying concerns about the biases that the group dynamic produces are only a problem when the individual's *private* views are the unit of analysis of interest (see, e.g., Hollander 2004, 610–611). Is the researcher interested in individual preferences, attitudes, or opinions? If so, then she should *not* use focus groups to collect data. It will not be an appropriate method precisely because of its social form.

Are Focus Group Findings Generalizable?

What about the second question? Specifically, are the data from focus groups representative of a larger group, such that what we learn from the focus group can inform a general theory (see, e.g., Babbie 1998)? The short answer is that they *can be* generalizable in theory, although it is difficult to do this in practice. Strictly speaking, it is not impossible to undertake the kind of probability sampling required to achieve generalizability (Fern 2001, 140). Depending on the population in question, however, a researcher may need to undertake near-heroic efforts to meet this requirement. For one randomized sampling is difficult to accomplish with focus groups and often not ideal for the research question at hand. Additionally, carrying out the number of focus groups necessary to achieve statistical representativeness is quite difficult and, again, often unnecessary. As we will see, it is rare for new data or ideas to be introduced after four to six focus groups, that is, with only about forty participants.

It is more realistic to recognize that focus groups are rarely the appropriate method to undertake when a researcher wishes to achieve generalization in the probabilistic sense.[2] For this kind of generalizability, a survey may be more

[2] On this point, there are also epistemological concerns to consider. If a researcher believes that focus groups create situated accounts – that is, an account unique to the moment and entirely subjective – then generalizability is not theoretically possible or desirable (see, e.g., Sim 1998, 349). Social scientists who do not adhere to the positivist paradigm tend to dismiss generalizability and validity as "folk notions" that do not apply to their work (Stoddart 2004; see also Babbie 1998). This text does not adopt this more phenomenological position, although you can find work on this perspective (see, e.g., Bradbury-Jones et al. 2008; Palmer et al. 2010).

appropriate. Instead, focus groups can be generalizable in the sense that what is learned about one group of individuals in a particular context can be **transferred** to other individuals in a similar context. The insights gleaned are transferrable precisely because of the comparability of context (Sim 1998, 349). Therefore, one can reasonably expect that the information that focus groups reveal about, for example, young widows or male breast cancer survivors will apply to other young widows or male breast cancer survivors. This is particularly the case where similar sentiments are expressed across multiple focus groups comprised of similar individuals.

Overall, what this section tells us is that it is difficult to remove the "group" from the "focus group." Group dynamics within the focus group are inevitable, although the problems these may cause can be mitigated. We have learned in this section that focus groups should not be used when researchers wish to access an individual's unmediated thoughts and opinions. They will also be of limited use when the researcher wishes to apply her findings beyond a particular subset of the population.

The Human Factor

As with any data collection method, the success of focus groups is dependent upon how they are organized, executed, and analyzed. It is dependent, in other words, on how carefully the researcher and the moderator fulfill their roles. We will discuss these roles in more detail in subsequent chapters, but the larger point does bear mentioning here: focus groups are vulnerable to human error.

Let us begin with focus group design – a topic we will explore in much more detail in Chapter 3. The careful organization of focus groups is essential to their success. We have seen above that focus groups are unique because they replicate particular social processes that give us insight into how individuals and groups think, act, and behave in the real world. Still, focus groups are not natural events. They would not occur on their own. Consequently, how and where they occur becomes quite important for effectively simulating real world processes. This means that focus groups must be "carefully managed," since their "naturalism" is contrived (Finch and Lewis 2003, 172; see also Bloor et al. 2001). The researcher's role is essential in achieving this naturalism. It means that she must not only develop a set of questions that will accurately tap into the research agenda (on this point, see Chapter 3). She must also identify a setting that will maximize participant comfort and ease.

Additionally, focus groups create a lot of data. It is not uncommon for one focus group to produce a transcript of more than twenty, single-spaced pages. This means that a researcher may realistically have to analyze dozens and dozens of pages of data to extract meaningful results from a set of focus groups.

Thanks to the open-ended nature of focus group questions, data analysis tends to be time-consuming and subject to significant interpretation (Stewart et al. 2009, 594–595). It is not an exaggeration to conclude, as Wells (1979) does, that a bad analyst will lead to a bad focus group report (p. 12, as taken from Stewart et al. 2009).

Overall, when it comes to focus group design and analysis, the role of the researcher is essential. Poor choices with respect to where and when focus groups will be held can impact the dynamic of the conversation that unfolds. Researchers must also adopt systematic practices when it comes to data analysis, a point we will revisit in Chapter 5. To be sure, the importance of design and analysis is not unique to focus groups. Still, one must work against the notion that focus groups are somehow "soft" when it comes to design, execution, and analysis (Copsey 2008, 3). Careful, justifiable choices on the part of the researcher can work against this characterization.

Finally, just as the researcher is responsible for successful focus group design and analysis, a moderator is vitally important for the effective execution of focus groups.[3] The moderator runs the focus group. She is responsible for asking the questions, following up on those questions where necessary, and managing the overall dynamic of the focus group conversation without leading or guiding the participants. These are no small tasks! Put simply, an inexperienced moderator can bias the results obtained (Stewart et al. 2009, 594–595). This is because the moderator must know to strike a balance between what the researcher finds important and what participants wish to address (Stewart et al. 2009, Chapter 3). She must work to extract sincere opinions and beliefs while fending off induced or false assertions (Lezuan 2007, 131). Overall, the moderator is in charge of managing the interactions through which focus group data are generated. Because of this, the moderator can make or break the data generating process (Morgan 1996).

The moderator is extremely important for focus group success. Therefore, proper training is essential. Chapter 3 provides pointers on how to effectively prepare the moderator for her role in the data collection method. For now, suffice it to say that, together with the researcher, the moderator is a potential source of human error when it comes to undertaking focus groups. One implication of this section is that focus groups may not be an appropriate data collection method when the researcher wishes to minimize human intervention in her

[3] In some research situations, the researcher herself serves as the moderator. While this approach is particularly helpful as a cost-saving measure, I nevertheless caution against this elision of the two roles. The moderator and the researcher, as we will see here and in Chapters 3 and 4, have quite a lot of distinct responsibilities when it comes to undertaking the focus group. It is, therefore, advisable to separate the two roles whenever possible. With that in mind, I treat the researcher and the moderator as two separate individuals throughout this text.

study. For that kind of work, ethnography or participant observation may be more appropriate.

The Costs Associated with Focus Groups

Finally, the execution of focus groups implies certain costs. On the one hand, they can be quite expensive, especially if the researcher relies on a consultancy firm to undertake them. Where this option is not available, then the researcher will expend quite a bit of time and energy undertaking the fairly extensive preparations that focus groups require. Still, the extent to which these preparations are much more time- or energy-demanding than other data collection methods, such as surveys or experiments, is an open question. We will revisit the material, time, and money required to prepare for focus groups in the next chapter. For now, keep in mind that, as with all data collection methods, when done correctly, focus groups imply certain costs to the researcher. They also imply certain tradeoffs. Still, as this chapter has suggested, they can be an incredibly useful and rich source of information for multiple types of research projects. The benefits derived from focus groups, in other words, will almost certainly outweigh their costs.

Conclusion

We have seen in this chapter that focus groups are an appropriate data collection method for addressing a variety of different research questions. We listed six different situations in which focus groups are particularly useful. They are helpful when considering social concepts, group processes and dynamics, and sensitive topics, as well as for contextualizing our research and/or exploring new topics.

Focus groups are also versatile. One can use them as a stand-alone method, in conjunction with other qualitative methods, and also alongside quantitative methods. This chapter has underscored the potential complementary uses of focus groups in a mixed-methods research design. Still, focus groups are clearly not appropriate for every research question. Especially when issues of statistical generalizability are a concern, or when individual attitudes/behaviors are the exclusive unit of interest, focus groups may not be ideal.

Overall, this chapter should have conveyed the multiple uses of focus groups and the unique kinds of information they can convey. Moving forward, we will move into the nuts and bolts of focus group-based research. It is time to move beyond *whether* to use focus groups for a particular research design and address *how* to use them. The next three chapters are dedicated to this task.

Exercises

2.1. A researcher wishes to measure what citizens understand as everyday acts of corruption in South America. She wants her findings to be generalizable while also sensitive to the different meanings that citizens may attach to corruption in, for example, Venezuela versus Argentina. What kind of research design would you recommend? Justify why your proposed research design will accomplish both of the researcher's goals (i.e. findings that are generalizable but also sensitive to context).

2.2. Examine the following set of research questions. Which ones might be appropriately addressed by focus groups? Which ones are best reserved for other data collection methods? Why?

- **a.** How do social pressures impact the self-worth of young women?
- **b.** What is the relationship between individual attitudes and political behavior?
- **c.** How does racism affect the everyday lives of minority groups?
- **d.** How much of an effect does religiosity have on voting preferences?

2.3. You wish to examine the effect of partisanship on civic engagement in the United States and Canada. You have designed and carried out a nationally representative survey in the United States on this question. Now you wish to apply the same survey to Canada. You are concerned, however, that certain questions may not easily translate from the US to the Canadian context. In particular, you are unsure about the kinds of civic engagement that are prevalent in Canada. How can focus groups help you address this uncertainty?

3 Preparing for the Focus Groups

This chapter, alongside Chapters 4 and 5, ventures into the practical terrain of carrying out focus groups. We will discuss, consecutively, the preparations that need to be done prior to the focus groups (Chapter 3); the steps involved with actually undertaking focus groups (Chapter 4); and the work associated with analyzing the data generated therein (Chapter 5). The following pages are therefore intended to provide the information that you need to be a successful focus group practitioner.

Toward that end, these chapters are comprehensive. They are also necessarily incomplete. No text will fully prepare you to address every potential challenge that can surface in the actual practice of data collection. As Barbour reminds us, "[t]here are . . . no hard-and-fast rules regarding the practicalities involved in planning and running focus groups" (2007, 90). Unexpected setbacks will occur. Unanticipated opportunities may arise. I do not, therefore, presume to provide an exhaustive rendering of focus group-based work. Instead, I hope to tackle the major issues and concerns that must be considered before, during, and after the focus groups have been undertaken, while providing you with the tools needed to carefully consider the implications of the (unexpected) decisions that you will likely need to make along the way.

This first, preparatory chapter is organized as follows. In the next section, I address the most important preparatory steps that you must take before heading into the space where your focus groups will be held. As I consider the nuts and bolts of focus group organization, I rely, where I can, upon a running example to help elucidate the decision-making process (Gamson 1992). Next, I pay close attention to two aspects of focus group work that are, arguably, vital to the data collection method's success. The first is the definition of the moderator and his/her preparation. This person is responsible for eliciting the responses that will comprise your data. The second is the making of the question protocol itself – the vessel, if you will, through which your data are generated. Choosing the moderator and developing a question protocol are essential steps in ensuring that your focus groups are as productive as possible. Because of this, they merit special treatment in the pages that follow.

Finally, I underscore some of the additional measures that should be considered when carrying out focus groups in non-native settings and on topics that may be considered sensitive or difficult to address. In these situations, the researcher and her moderator should take extra care to be cognizant of cultural norms and sensitivities, power differentials, especially between the moderator and the participants, and other preparatory details that may not be necessary in settings that are familiar to the researcher and over topics that are not expected to be controversial. Focus groups are especially well suited for these kinds of situations, but they do require additional care in their preparation.

The Nuts and Bolts of Undertaking Focus Groups

The point of departure of any successful data collection endeavor is the research question driving the project. This point cannot be overstated. When a researcher decides to carry out focus groups, it is presumed that the research question has been clearly defined, the relevant population has been identified, and existing information on the topic has been obtained and absorbed (Stewart et al. 2007, 53–54). Chapters 1 and 2 offered a set of guidelines for determining the kinds of questions that focus groups are well suited to address. My assumption moving forward, therefore, is that you – as the future focus group practitioner – have already decided that focus groups make sense for your particular research question.

With that decision behind you, you now face a set of logistical quandaries. With whom will you carry out focus groups? How many focus groups should you organize? Where should they take place? What kinds of questions should you ask? Who should ask the questions? Where, in other words, do you begin?

Before initiating any of the logistical footwork, it makes sense to first answer a set of questions regarding certain practicalities of focus group organization (see Table 3.1). These answers will help you establish a "wish list," or a logistical plan that represents how you would carry out focus groups in the most ideal of circumstances. In practice, you will likely find that many of your

Table 3.1 Practical Questions about Focus Groups

1. How many focus groups should I carry out?
2. What is my sampling frame?
3. What should the composition of each focus group be?
4. How should I recruit participants?
5. Will I work with a research consultancy?
6. Where will the focus groups occur?
7. What materials should I prepare?
8. How will I record the conversation?
9. What costs should I expect?
10. Do I need consent?
11. Who will be my moderator?
12. What questions will I ask?

ideals are difficult to meet. Nevertheless, by specifying a preferred starting point, you will be better equipped to make and later explain certain decisions that were less than optimal.

Focus Group Composition and Recruitment (Questions 1 to 6)

The first questions you must ask are fairly broad: How many focus groups should I carry out? Additionally, who should speak on the questions I have? What is the appropriate group (or groups) to speak on the subject? What, in other words, is my population of interest (sometimes called a *sampling frame*) for this research question?

How Many Focus Groups Should I Carry Out? (Question 1)

Regarding the number of focus groups, this will vary according to the research question and the desired composition of the focus groups. Generally speaking, with four to six focus groups a researcher will arrive at data saturation, that is, the point after which the introduction of new, relevant data is increasingly rare. As a general rule of thumb, then, a maximum of six focus groups should be the goal (Morgan 1996). Still, a researcher may wish to access multiple perspectives from different stakeholders on a particular topic of interest. For example, when addressing the effectiveness of a particular addiction treatment program, a researcher may wish to speak to addicts and also to the counselors responsible for administering the treatment. In this case, the researcher may aim to carry out, for example, four focus groups with each group (i.e., addicts and counselors).[1]

What Is My Sampling Frame? (Question 2)

The **sampling frame** represents the list of people, households, organizations, or groups that the researcher believes is a good approximation of the research population of interest (Stewart et al. 2007, 45). Before beginning data collection, a researcher must first define the sampling frame to which her research question applies. Once defined, she then can develop a strategy for recruitment that entails capturing as representative a sample of that population as possible.

Certainly, researchers must take great care in identifying the appropriate population(s) from which to recruit focus group participants. Here, the research question is key. It helps determine, first, with whom a researcher

[1] When planning focus groups, costs are an important consideration. I address this point in greater detail below.

would like to speak and, second, whether or not she would like to speak to more than one group or population. Let us return to the example of the addiction treatment program above. A research question might be: How effective is treatment X perceived to be in comparison with previous addiction treatments? On this point, addicts and counselors will likely offer different (but equally consequential) reactions on treatment effectiveness. Therefore, the researcher may wish to identify two sampling frames (addicts *and* counselors) and plan for recruitment accordingly. Given the comparative nature of the research question, the researcher will want to locate, where possible, addicts and counselors that have had experience with *both* treatment X and at least one previous treatment.

How, then, does one identify these individuals? And what is the best way to recruit individuals once they have been identified? Let's tackle this question by examining, first, how one research team actually identified and recruited a set of focus group participants. We can, then, develop a set of conclusions based on their experience. Box 3.1 introduces a project undertaken by William A. Gamson. The project included multiple focus groups and was published in the 1992 book, *Talking Politics*.

As Box 3.1 shows, Gamson was successful in carrying out multiple focus groups. Importantly, tradeoffs were made when it came to the sampling and recruitment process. For one, Gamson ultimately decided to truncate his sampling frame to the Boston area. Truncation inherently limits the generalizability of his results. This means the conclusions are less likely to apply to groups outside the Boston area. Geographical delimitation also, however, gave Gamson more control over the recruitment process, as he could use his own knowledge as a resident of Boston to achieve considerable diversity within the city limits.

Second, Gamson sought to compose each focus group with a diverse group of individuals. Yet, his recruitment strategy – his team recruited one individual who would then enlist the remaining participants in a particular group – meant that the focus groups tended to stratify into all white or all black groups. Overall, then, the focus groups were racially homogenous, if also heterogeneous in terms of sex and age.

What Should the Composition of Each Focus Group Be? (Question 3)

Certainly, composition matters for focus groups. The goals of your project can help you define the ideal make up of each group. A research question, for example, might seek to understand whether gender affects notions of equality. Here, the researcher will likely organize all male and all female focus groups. Generally speaking, the researcher should carefully consider the scope and

Box 3.1 A Running Example: *Talking Politics*

In his book, *Talking Politics* (1992), William A. Gamson examines how people construct meaning about politics. He is specifically interested in understanding how individuals discuss particular, hot-button issues when left to their own devices. He asks, what frames do citizens use to make sense of complicated topics? He is particularly interested in understanding how exposure to the mass media might affect the frames citizens use. He therefore further asks, how does mass media consumption affect how citizens understand complicated issues?

To help answer this question, Gamson organized several focus groups, through which he could speak with citizens directly. He ended up organizing thirty-seven focus groups comprised of a total of 188 participants (an average of about five individuals per focus group). He chose to exclude college students or graduates from his population, as he was interested in how working people in particular – individuals who "do not own the means of production, who sell their labor power to others" (Gamson 1992, 14) – processed the news and understood politics.

Data collection was undertaken in the Boston area, a choice that made sense logistically even though it limited the extent to which the results could be generalized (Gamson 1992, 15). The groups varied in terms of race, gender, religion, and age, though of the thirty-seven focus groups, only three were interracial. Seventeen were all white, and seventeen were all black. Recruitment occurred in multiple sites. The author chose to focus on "public sites," where a recruitment table would not be overly conspicuous, including during the festivals, picnics, fairs, and markets that occurred in different communities (Gamson 1992, 16). His intention was to recruit one person who would then recruit friends or colleagues to complete the group.

conditions of the research question under investigation. Given its content, with whom would you ideally speak? Which groups, organizations, or individuals would be best poised to answer the question? Are there distinctions that are vital? If so, then these should be prioritized when it comes to recruitment. Secondary goals – for example, Gamson's desire to achieve as much heterogeneity as possible – may be sought as well, but a research question can still be answered if those goals are not fully met. Overall, it is best to keep in mind that group composition affects the answers that you will get.

Researchers must make additional considerations when it comes to focus group composition. Should, for example, they be comprised of strangers or acquaintances? Gamson deliberately chose to work with peer groups. When focus groups include acquaintances, conversations may unfold more easily, such that underlying patterns of meaning are more easily uncovered (Flick 2009, 197). Nonetheless, the researcher should be cognizant of how sensitive the topic might be. Friendly neighbors may not be as willing to address complicated and potentially polarizing topics, such as teen pregnancy, drug use, or religious beliefs. Tensions may emerge that may make future interactions less comfortable. With strangers, the longer-term effects of the tensions that conversations might reveal will be less consequential. Alternatively, it may be more difficult to get the conversational "ball" rolling – although in my experience, if the questions are topical enough, citizens will want to talk.

Additionally, as with Gamson's project, a researcher will have to decide how homogenous a group should be, as well as in what way. For certain questions (e.g., the differential effect of a new drug addiction treatment), homogeneity will be preferred. Participants, such as drug addicts or counselors, will have a lot in common – a sense of solidarity and shared experience – that can make sharing easier. This sense of solidarity is especially ideal when studying sensitive topics, such as drug addiction, sexual assault, or racial discrimination (Finch et al. 2014, 231; Liamputtong 2011). With homogenous groups, it will also be easier to compare data collected *across* multiple focus groups. Alternatively, when groups are homogenous, it may be difficult to tease out difference or disagreement among participants.

With more heterogeneous groups, a researcher may wish to exploit differences in opinion or reaction within a single group setting. One should be careful, however, to avoid bringing together individuals with socio-demographic differences that may be particularly pronounced, for example, mixing class or age groups that are obviously very different. Here, diversity can make people uncomfortable and impede, rather than fuel, conversations (Finch et al. 2014, 231). For example, in focus groups about pregnancy termination, a researcher can attempt to achieve diversity in terms of age and relationship status, but she may wish to only include women who have had abortions.

Note the use of the term, "attempt," in the previous sentence. It is important to keep in mind that our expectations regarding group composition – as with all things regarding focus group preparations – should be realistic. Some group distinctions (or similarities) will be necessary for the focus groups we organize. Others, however, might be ideal but ultimately secondary for the research question at hand. When it comes to group composition, therefore, researchers should identify those differences or similarities that must be leveraged. Beyond that, however, the researcher may have to cede some control over the actual groups that form.[2]

[2] The researcher must, ultimately, take group composition into account when analyzing the data collected. On this point, asking participants to fill out a demographic questionnaire will be helpful. More on this below.

Recruiting your Participants; Working with Professionals; and Identifying a Space for Undertaking Focus Groups (Questions 4, 5, and 6)

Understanding your priorities for focus group composition is vital for a successful recruitment process. It is also a very difficult undertaking. This is especially the case if you do not have the resources to hire a consultancy group to do the recruitment for you. For some authors, recruitment represents "the single most common source of failure" in undertaking focus groups (Morgan 1995, 517). There are many reasons for this. For one, achieving the desired focus group composition can be very difficult. Additionally, restrictions imposed by your Institutional Review Board (IRB, see below) may limit where and how you recruit potential participants. Finally, and perhaps most importantly, though you may feel quite confident that you have successfully recruited enough participants, you can never know *for sure* that individuals will actually show up to the designated place at the designated time.

Recruitment is, therefore, both vital to a successful data collection process and also extremely difficult to control (Morgan 1995; see also Krueger and Casey 2015). The best one can do is develop a recruitment strategy that you feel will maximize the likelihood of success. First and foremost, you must think carefully about "where and how potential group members spend their time, what barriers may exist that make participation difficult, and what incentives are valued by the group" (Stewart et al. 2007, 59). The answers to these questions should help you identify *where* recruitment should happen; *how* recruitment can best take place; and even *when* and *where* the actual focus groups should take place.

Recruitment should happen, quite simply, in those places where your ideal group members spend their time. Might they belong to the same church or civil society organization? Is there a public space (e.g., a park or a plaza) that they typically frequent? Gamson sought to recruit a wide diversity of people from multiple different communities (see Box 3.1). He therefore zeroed in on public events in those targeted communities. Note that he explicitly chose *not* to recruit at public events that were political in nature. He did not want to bias his sample toward individuals who could be politically inclined (Gamson 1992, 16).

Once you identify where recruitment will happen, you must decide how actually to recruit. Will you set up a recruitment table, as Gamson (1992) did? Will you enlist the help of church or civil society organization volunteers? Engaging the peers of your potential participants can be extremely useful for successful recruitment. When utilizing the help of others, however, you must consider the following. First, your IRB must approve of whatever approach you devise. Second, you must properly train your enlisted volunteers on what they must (not) say when recruiting participants. For example, they may need to ask screening questions to gauge whether an individual meets your specified requirements. You may want them to briefly describe the kinds of conversations that will take place in the focus group. Perhaps they can mention, as Gamson did, that compensation will be provided. Once these decisions have been made, keep in mind that you should then *over*-recruit by at least 20 to 25 percent. Better to have too many rather than too few participants show up (on this problem, see Chapter 4).

Some researchers may have access to a consultancy group with whom they can work to recruit participants and even, in some cases, carry out the focus groups. The clear advantage to this is that a researcher will ostensibly be working with a person or team with a demonstrated record in undertaking focus groups. They will likely have a recruitment process to which they can tailor your research needs. They may also have a place where the focus groups can take place. If this type of assistance is within your reach, then I recommend grasping it with both hands! The problem, of course, is that this kind of professional help tends to be expensive. If you have the money, then you should do your due diligence. Speak with more than one consultancy group near your research site. Request estimates for the work to be undertaken. Negotiate. Re-negotiate. Then, make the best decision given your project.

Finally, the decision regarding where and how to recruit may impact your choices on when and where to host the focus group conversations. Is there a space available in the civil society organization or church in question? Is there a quiet café or restaurant near the public space where recruitment occurred? You will want to identify a location and a time that is convenient to your population of interest. This means establishing a time out of regular work hours and choosing a space that they can easily access.

In addition to convenience, you want to identify a space that is large enough to comfortably fit the six to ten individuals you have recruited plus a moderator, yourself, a table and chairs, and the equipment you will use to record the conversations. You also want to identify a *quiet* space where interruptions will, ideally, be minimized. Data collection will be much more difficult if participants cannot hear each other and your recording equipment cannot hear the participants. Some creativity may be required when it comes to identifying an appropriate space. You should rely on your knowledge of the research site, and the knowledge of others when possible, to make this step as painless as possible.

The Material Needs of Focus Groups (Questions 7 and 8)

To be sure, identifying a *space* for hosting the focus groups is but one of several material demands that focus groups require. Focus groups are quite material intensive. When you show up on the day of the focus group(s), you should keep in mind that you typically must arrive with the following items:

1. **Recording equipment**. Most principally, you will need to tape the focus group conversations. This is indispensable for the transcription process. You may choose to audio- or videotape the focus groups. There are trade-offs to videotaping the focus group. On the one hand, you can more easily keep track of who is speaking and also capture the non-verbal responses that can be so central to content analysis. On the other, the presence of a video camera may make your participants uncomfortable. It will also have greater implications for the kind of consent that your IRB may require, since anonymity will be harder to protect when visual data are created alongside the audio data. In my experience, audiotaping works just fine, especially if you, as the researcher, can keep track of particularly important non-verbal inflections and participant order in your own, written notes. Regardless of the recording mode, be sure to bring the device's charger or an extra battery, in the event that an outlet is not immediately accessible. If your focus groups take place outside of your home country, keep in mind the voltage and outlet requirements of the research site and plan to bring any converting devices that may be necessary. (In fact, you should make note of these technological requirements in an on-site visit *before* the day of the focus groups, to prevent any potential technological issues.)
2. **Pens, paper, name-tags, envelopes**. Many focus groups ask participants to write down certain answers or thoughts before sharing them. For this, writing implements and paper will be necessary. It is also typically nice to provide name-tags, so that you, the moderator, and other participants can easily refer to everyone's first name as the conversation unfolds. Depending on your IRB's consenting procedures, you may need to enclose consent forms and demographic questionnaires in sealed envelopes, so be sure to bring these along as well.
3. **Consent forms, demographic questionnaires**. Often, participants fill out a demographic questionnaire before (or after) a focus group takes place. You may also need to obtain the written consent of your participants before the focus group can take place. Bring these forms with you! Of course, this seems obvious, but often it is the obvious things that we take for granted – and, consequently, leave behind or forget – in the final days leading up to the focus groups.
4. **Compensation**. Researchers often compensate focus group participants for their time (more on this below). It is best to have the compensation, however defined, divvied up, ready to disseminate, and stored with the consent forms and demographic questionnaires prior to the focus group(s).

5. **Refreshments**. It is customary to provide your participants with some light refreshments (e.g., a beverage or two, cookies or crackers) to enjoy before, during, and after the focus group. In addition to the drinks and food, remember to bring enough cups, plates, and napkins for your expected participants.
6. **Table, chairs**. Ideally, your defined space for the focus groups will come equipped with the furniture where focus group participants, the moderator, and you will sit. In the absence of this infrastructure, you will need to provide it yourself. Keep in mind that, in addition to the space needed for different individuals, you will need room for the refreshments and also for your recording equipment.

The Costs Associated with Focus Groups (Question 9)

Focus groups are not cost-free. Still, the financial commitment required can vary depending on how resourceful you are during focus group preparations. For example, the researcher may directly purchase many of the material needs listed above. She can rent a space; buy the paper goods; pay for photocopies; and purchase the refreshments at a local market. She may also, however, utilize a donated or borrowed space and/or acquire the paper goods from, and make the photocopies with, a local institutional host. Focus groups, in other words, need not exert *excessive* costs if the researcher is willing to do the footwork necessary to reduce certain expenditures.

Still, certain costs will likely be unavoidable. For one, it is customary to pay your moderator for his/her time and experience. The rate should be negotiated and adjusted both for the level of the moderator's previous experience and typical moderator rates in the area. The participants also often receive monetary compensation (although this is not always the case, see Box 3.2). Even if the cost per person is relatively low (say, $5 to $10 per person), the overall expense can nevertheless become quite high, especially if you organize six focus groups with ten people each (a grand total of $300 to $600).

Finally, researchers should keep in mind the costs involved with transcribing the focus group conversations. Certainly, there are financial costs to this step. These can be curtailed somewhat, however, if you can "outsource" transcription to a third party. For example, an undergraduate research assistant may charge less per hour than a graduate assistant or professional. Additionally, it may be wise, both financially and analytically, to have a native transcribe your data if your focus groups took place in another country. Hourly rates may be lower. Moreover, that person may be better equipped to decipher colloquialisms and other local linguistic idiosyncrasies.

Box 3.2 What/How Much Compensation should Participants Receive?

It is customary to provide focus group participants with compensation of some kind in exchange for the time and energy they contribute to the focus group (Bloor et al. 2001). Quite often, researchers provide a monetary award. In this case, one must decide how much money is appropriate. Often, researchers take into consideration the travel costs incurred in arriving at the data collection site and time potentially missed in a job or additional commitment (Hennink 2007, 31–32).

Researchers must be careful, however, to balance a desire to compensate for time with what may be perceived as a monetary inducement to participate at all.

Additionally, in some cases (e.g., as with upper class participants), a relatively small monetary prize may not be appropriate. Instead, a researcher might donate the total of the group's "earned" money to a charity or an organization of choice.

Indeed, where monetary compensation is not preferred, researchers may think creatively to offer alternative forms of compensation. For example, all participants may be entered into a lottery, in which one or two prizes (e.g., a tablet or a gift certificate) are included. This may be preferable from a price stand point, as one or two non-monetary gifts may be less expensive than a universal cash handout.

Ultimately, any decision regarding compensation must be approved by your institution's IRB. That said, there is some flexibility (and creativity!) involved in devising the compensation structure that works for your project.

In addition to the financial costs, the researcher must also keep in mind the labor and time involved in transcription. This is not an easy (or particularly fun) process! Finding a trusted third party can alleviate the burdens of this intensive and extremely important step in the data collection process. On this last point, a researcher who has the funds may wish to hire a local consultancy firm to carry out the entire data collection process from start (i.e., recruitment) to finish (i.e., transcription). This will likely be the most costly budgetary item to consider, and so it is not typically available to most social science researchers.

Overall, resource-strapped researchers may wish to think carefully about where they will invest the limited funds they have when it comes to doing focus groups. Personally, I find that the most difficult, time-consuming, and labor-intensive aspect of the focus group process is transcribing the data collected onto paper. I therefore prioritize, above all else, allaying these costs. Then, I decide how to distribute my remaining funds. Ultimately, it is important to keep in mind that the money you have at your disposal, together with your resourcefulness and contacts on the ground, will determine how many focus groups you can feasibly carry out. Consequently, this is not a step in your focus group preparations that should be taken lightly.

The Institutional Review Board (IRB) Process (Question 10)

The IRB represents a group of individuals at an academic institution that has been designated to review and monitor all research involving human subjects. Its primary purpose is to ensure that the rights and welfare of the humans involved in any research project are protected. The IRB is charged with reviewing the protocols and related materials associated with a given research project, such that human rights and welfare are preserved.[3]

Most researchers are subject to some form of IRB oversight and/or approval prior to carrying out focus group-based research. This oversight can present certain limits regarding how and where participant recruitment occurs, including what can(not) be said, as well as whether, and what kind of, consent is needed. Generally speaking, the IRB will review all documents associated with a data collection project, including recruitment scripts, question protocols, questionnaires, and/or sign-up sheets. The path to IRB approval can be fairly circuitous. Importantly, the requirements and restrictions vary from institution to institution (Stark 2011). Therefore, I recommend that you present your preferred focus group project to the IRB and adjust it according to their response.

Choosing and Training the Moderator (Question 11)

Thus far we have addressed, with some brevity, some important considerations involved in focus group preparation. In the next two sections of this chapter, we will spend more time addressing two final aspects of the focus group that must be carefully considered prior to undertaking focus groups: choosing a moderator and developing the question protocol. These two concerns deserve more attention, because they are truly crucial for the overall success of the focus groups. For one, the questions help determine the kinds of topics covered throughout the conversation. The moderator, in turn, is largely responsible for eliciting responses and, consequently, nurturing and guiding the conversations taking place. Taken together, the set of questions and the

[3] See www.fda.gov/RegulatoryInformation/Guidances/ucm126420.htm (last accessed July 24, 2018), for more information. Information on human research standards in other countries is available at: www.hhs.gov/ohrp/international/compilation-human-research-standards/index.html (last accessed August 9, 2018)

moderator condition, in great part, the nature and the quality of the data generated.

Let us first examine the role of the moderator. This person conducts the focus group from start to finish, introducing the topics of interest, regulating the tenor and flow of the discussions that take place, and ensuring that all participants are both at ease and engaged. Depending on the question protocol, a moderator may also have to present stimulus material (e.g., a newspaper article, a video, an audio clip) and/or engage participants in a specific activity, such as a team-building or brainstorming exercise (Onwuegbuzie et al. 2009, 4).

The moderator should also keep track of points raised that may need to be revisited, while simultaneously regulating the dynamic of the group itself. She may have to draw out shy or quiet participants or discourage dominant or disruptive ones – tasks that require a certain level of empathy and tactical flexibility (Morrison-Beedy et al. 2001, 50). Finally, moderators must be sensitive to the nature of their own participation in the focus group. On this point, a "delicate balance" is required (Sim 1998, 347). The moderator must be engaged to stimulate participation while also sufficiently removed from the conversation so as not to stymie its flow. In short, moderating is no small task!

In a focus group comprised of professional focus group moderators, participants identified the ideal set of skills one should have to thrive in their line of work: personality, sensitivity, insight, ability, empathy, warmth, and listening and analytical skills (Caruso 1976, as taken from Fern 2001, 75).

Given the rather hefty role that a moderator must fulfill, it behooves the researcher to spend some time electing the appropriate person to oversee her focus groups. Indeed, the literature tells us that, in choosing a moderator, certain traits are desirable. A moderator should be empathetic, genuinely interested in what others say, animated and spontaneous, flexible, eloquent, and have a sense of humor (Stewart et al. 2007, 79). Good interpersonal skills, in general, are important, since the moderator has a powerful influence on the conversations that take place (Sim 1998, 347).

In addition to these desired personality traits, a moderator's gender or race can be important. For example, a researcher might wish to have a woman moderate a set of focus groups comprised of women who have experienced sexual assault. When carrying out focus groups in another country, a researcher might consider working with a native speaker – someone familiar with local speech patterns. In his focus groups, Gamson (1992) matched the race of the moderator with that of his focus group participants. Given the topic of the focus groups, these demographic considerations may be minor. Keep in mind, however, that the chosen moderator should be someone with whom focus group participants can relate and/or feel comfortable (Fern 2001, 75).

Finally, when possible, researchers should choose an individual with previous moderating experience. While inexperience is not necessarily an impediment to successful moderation, a first-time moderator may be unwilling to allow a conversation to deviate too much from the question protocol – a tendency that can inhibit spontaneous conversation (Kidd and Parshall 2000, 294). Less experienced moderators may also, consciously or not, wish to please the researcher, inadvertently seeking to confirm hypotheses and steering participants away from alternative positions (Stewart et al. 2007, 85).

Of course, one's moderator "wish list" may not be fully realized. Where this occurs, take heart! If one's choice of moderator is suboptimal, the researcher may nevertheless find solace in the fact that focus groups are remarkably "robust" to any potential moderator weaknesses (Morgan 1995, 521). Indeed, the researcher will spend considerable time and energy training the moderator prior to overseeing any focus group. Therefore, she can exercise a certain amount of control over how the moderator functions in practice. Let us, then, conclude this section by discussing moderator preparation.

When preparing your moderator, it is important to keep in mind both the nature of the research question at hand, as well as the group dynamics that might arise given group composition and the questions to be discussed (Stewart et al. 2007, 81). How, then, does one train a person to moderate? I recommend meeting at least once (if not more) with your chosen moderator. Explain the motivations for organizing the focus groups. Introduce the primary research question(s). On this point, be careful not to reveal your expectations or hypotheses, since this can bias the moderator toward drawing out certain responses.

Next, consider the question protocol in its entirety and develop a strategy for addressing each question. To do this, make sure, first, that the moderator understands each question. (This is especially important in non-native contexts, where phrasing or content may not "travel" as well as the researcher might think.) Then, explain the goal behind each question. Note that this is different from explaining the desired or hypothesized response that you suspect a question will elicit. For example, it might be useful for you to explain that you want a question to elicit an emotional response (e.g., "With this question, I want to understand how *x* makes them feel."). You may also instruct the moderator *not* to use certain cues or words unless first addressed by the participants themselves. Here, your goal is to ensure that the moderator adopts the appropriate tone and guides the discussion in an appropriate way, without inadvertently leading participants toward a particular response or outcome. In the past, I have found it useful to make certain instructions explicit on the question protocol that I give to the moderator. I then encourage the moderator to study these instructions, essentially memorizing them before overseeing the first focus group (see Appendix 1 for an example).

Finally, you may wish to provide specific instructions regarding the moderator's overall approach to the conversations. You may, for example, encourage reflective listening, wherein the moderator clarifies, summarizes, and paraphrases certain points along the way so as to prevent miscommunication or misunderstanding (Fern 2001, 81–82). You should also remind the moderator to avoid making any kind of verbal or non-verbal judgments. Focus group participants should feel free to speak openly and honestly. Finally, a moderator may be instructed to gently engage with shy or reticent participants. She should also know to – again, gently – frustrate the attempts of participants who are particularly dominant or disruptive. I spell out some strategies on how to deal with challenging participants in the next chapter.

One last point to keep in mind. It will be useful to address your expectations regarding how much control the moderator exerts over the focus group conversation. You may ask the moderator to prevent participants from straying too far from the topic at hand. This might be ideal for comparative purposes. Greater imposition will allow for better standardization across focus groups (Morgan 1996). However, where the research is more exploratory in nature, it may be useful to instruct the moderator to intervene only minimally in conversations.

In his project, Gamson (1992) instructed his moderators to exert more control. He instructed them to break off contact as soon as (politely) possible with any one participant and to encourage others to join the conversation. They were told to avoid reacting, to the extent possible, to comments participants made. Moderators were instructed to keep participants on track in terms of the topic at hand, although what counted as "off track" was defined quite narrowly, so as to encourage participants to bring in their own experiences (Gamson 1992, 17–18).

Training the moderator is, therefore, of utmost importance when it comes to focus group preparations. Indeed, the care you take in preparing your moderator will likely be reflected in the quality of the focus groups that ultimately take place. As a final recommendation, I suggest that you take the time to write down the logic behind your choice of moderator. You should make note of her preferred demographic profile. You should also write down the specific instructions that you gave prior to the focus groups. There are two reasons for this. First, you should be prepared to make your moderating choices public, in the interests of methodological transparency. Second, you might need to carry out more focus groups in the future – sometimes, well into the future.

In my case, thanks to funding and other resource constraints, three years passed between two rounds of fieldwork for a single project (Cyr 2017b). If I had not carefully made note of my instruction protocol and moderator choices, I would have had reason to be concerned about the comparability across each set of focus groups.

Defining the Question Protocol (Question 12)

Developing a set of questions, sometimes called a question protocol or a questioning route, may seem easier than it actually is. In fact, a lot of careful consideration is required. For one, a researcher must strategize over the best use of the focus group's fairly limited length. In one and a half to two hours – the standard time of any single focus group – you will be hard-pressed to ask more than eight to twelve questions (Krueger 1998a). Ask more than that, and you will sacrifice the substantive depth that makes focus groups so unique as a method.

Questions, then, should be carefully thought out, with an emphasis on making the most of a limited time frame. They must also be pointed, that is, directed toward the research at hand. Finally, they should be engaging for the participants and even fun. In all, writing a question protocol is no easy task! Therefore, this section is oriented toward helping you create a useful set of focus group questions.

Above all else, when developing your focus group questions, you must keep your research goals in mind. What are you hoping to learn from the participants? What topics do you want them to address? The questions should evoke conversation, but they should also be one-dimensional. That is, each question should address one issue or topic. It is better to ask two questions, addressing two different dimensions of an issue (How was the program useful to you? How was it practical?), rather than fold both into one (How was the program useful and practical?). Overall, the questions should be concise and easy to understand. Ideally, they will adopt the language and idioms of the participants themselves (Krueger and Casey 2015, Chapter 3).

When developing a question protocol, most obviously, the questions should be open-ended in nature. If questions can be answered with a simple, "yes" or "no," then they are unlikely to generate much conversation. In Gamson's study, for example, the moderator asked participants to think about issues that were prominent in the news cycle at that time. She asked, "When you think about this issue of . . ., what comes to mind?" (Gamson 1992, 194–195). Phrased as such, citizens are invited to give their reaction, whatever it might be, to the topic.

Keep in mind that it may even be advisable to avoid "why" questions, as they can inadvertently put individuals on the defensive. Rather than ask, for example, why your participants participated in a particular program, you might consider rephrasing it in the following way: "What prompted you to participate in . . .?" (Krueger et al. 2001, 9). In the case of Gamson's project, a follow-up prompt to the initial issue-based question mentioned above might not be "Why did you have that reaction?" Instead, the moderator should be prompted to react, where appropriate, "That is interesting. What do you think causes you to have that reaction?"

Additionally, the kinds of questions you ask can (and should!) vary. For example, it may be appropriate to ask questions that compel participants to recall an experience or event – presumably, one that is related to the research question at hand. You might also use visual aids, stories, song lyrics, or advertisements to contextualize a particular question. Returning to Gamson (1992), the participants were presented with a political cartoon that tackled the same issue they had previously discussed. Here, participants were asked to comment on the cartoon specifically. These questions break up the monotony and engage participants in a different way (Krueger 1998a). Along these lines, participants may be asked listing, rating, or sorting questions, where they are asked to work together to categorize or classify a set of topics related to the research (Colucci 2007).

Note that the inclusion of a non-standard or traditional question can be a useful tactic for asking the same question in a different way. This strategy – asking a similar question in multiple formats – allows a researcher to check for the reliability of participant responses on certain, key questions. In most focus group research designs, the researcher will be particularly interested in assessing participant reactions to one or two driving concerns. Often these concerns are the justification for the focus groups themselves.

For example, I have used focus groups to understand why certain Peruvians identify strongly with or against a particularly controversial former leader, Alberto Fujimori. At the time of the research, not much was known about these individuals, who often identify as *fujimoristas* or anti-*fujimoristas*. I organized focus groups of either *fujimoristas* or anti-*fujimoristas* to understand how they thought about each group and why they identified as belonging to one or the other. I asked several questions to tap into the same notion: How individuals understand the meaning of "(anti-)fujimorista." One question included a group exercise, which required participants to work together and list the traits of an ideal politician. The purpose of this question allowed me to assess, first, whether that politician reflected the qualities that they associated with (anti-)*fujimorismo*, and, second, the extent to which there was agreement about what (anti-)*fujimorismo* was.

Finally, it may be appropriate periodically to ask participants to write down their response on a particular question before voicing it to the rest of the group. There are two benefits to this. Most importantly, it can allow you, as the researcher, to check for the presence of group think (see Chapter 4) or of an overly influential participant. Do participants' vocal responses cohere with what they wrote? If so, then you can feel more confident that their spoken answers were not overly swayed by one particularly predominant idea or person. Additionally, a written record of certain responses may be useful when it comes to analyzing your data. When, for example, measuring how participants understand their (anti-)*fujimorista* identity, it was useful for me to ask each participant to assign three characteristics to that identity. The primary goal was to spark a group conversation about the characteristics that were listed. As a secondary objective, however, I sought to glean an actual count of the different descriptors used by participants and the extent to which they assigned the same descriptor to the identity. The written responses were useful in crafting a database on this point. They also allowed me to analyze data created at the individual level of analysis (see, e.g., Chapter 5).

Keep in mind that your research goals will also shape the question protocol. What do you wish to learn from the focus groups? Is the project largely exploratory in nature? Are you hoping to test a hypothesis? The goals of the research will help determine the kinds of questions you ask. This, of course, seems obvious. In a focus group about drug addiction, it will not make sense to pose questions about political preferences. Less obvious, however, is that your research goals can even influence the *number* of questions you ask. For instance, when your goal is largely exploratory, it may make sense to ask only one or two very open questions. When, however, your goal is to test a theory or hypothesis, it makes more sense to develop a full question guide with fairly structured questions (Morrison-Beedy et al. 2001, 48).

Finally, as with most things methodological, there are tradeoffs involved with crafting a usable question protocol. For one, questions should be open enough to generate discussion. Yet, there is also some utility to retaining and, where necessary, imposing the order and nature of the question protocol. This is especially true where you expect to compare responses across focus groups. Greater focus group standardization will make comparability feasible. At the same time, too much standardization can expose focus groups to the "fallacy of adhering to fixed questions" (Morgan 1996, 142). After all, participants may wish to take the conversation in a different direction than the questions allow. One possible solution to this tradeoff is to pre-test and/or run a pilot of the questions with one or two focus groups to see if the general tenor of the conversation veers too much from the protocol itself. This requires time and resources, however, which the researcher may not have. An alternative solution would be to establish a small set of core questions that must be asked and allow for greater flexibility beyond that (Morgan 1996).

The researcher may also wish to strategize about the best approach to question order. Sometimes it may make sense to begin with a general question and make each additional question increasingly pointed, such that the final questions address the researcher's most important concerns. This sequencing can allow participants to flex their "focus group muscles," if you will, before getting to the really crucial questions. It may also, however, generate participant fatigue and inadvertently constrain the quality of the discussion of those important questions. On this point, question variety can mitigate fatigue. Additionally, where the researcher hopes to ask the same (ostensibly important) question twice, she may place one version closer to the beginning of the focus group and the other nearer to the end.

Indeed, as a final note of caution, the researcher must keep the overall flow of the conversation in mind when devising a set of questions. Is the question order relatively seamless, such that one question is followed by a different but not unrelated question? If not, then the researcher may wish to allow for some sort of transition text, whereby the moderator explains where the group has been, figuratively speaking, and where they are going. This way, the turn from one topic to another is less disjointed.

Certainly, it makes sense to begin the focus group with an opening question. This question is easy and quick to answer. It is designed to get everyone talking from the get-go. Next, you may want to ask an introductory question – one related to the primary topic of interest but still pretty general in nature. This question serves to break the ice, introducing the participants to the topic without requiring them to engage too directly or specifically with the primary research concerns. From here, you may wish to include a transition question – one that brings the participants to the "heart" of the discussion. This would be followed by the key questions of interest, the figurative "heart" of your investigative inquiry. Finally, time permitting, you may wish to close the focus group with a reflective question, one that allows the participants to summarize their contribution and perhaps speculate about some future aspect of the topic at hand (Krueger and Casey 2015, Chapter 3). Box 3.3 provides a sample question protocol from a project on Venezuelan political parties that follows this format.

Question choices clearly matter when it comes to preparing your focus group design. Knowing what you want to ask, how and when you wish to ask it, and where there might be wiggle room along the way will greatly facilitate a successful focus group experience. To be sure, understanding

Box 3.3 Sample Question Protocol (see also Appendix 1)

1. (Opening question) As I mentioned earlier, we hope to learn a bit about your impressions of different political parties in Venezuela. Before we jump into the questions, however, I'd like each of you to tell us a bit about yourself. Please tell us your first name. Then, give us a sense of how interested you are in politics. Would you say that you spend a lot of time (maybe even daily!), some time, or not very much time thinking about politics?
2. (Introductory question) Now that we know each other, I want to start off with a bit of a memory exercise. Specifically, I'd like to ask you all to think back to the late 1990s. As you probably recall, in 1998, Hugo Chávez was elected to office in a fairly momentous election. At that time, two parties (AD and COPEI) were elected out of office. I would like each of you to think back to that period and tell us a story about AD that you remember. It can be an anecdote about a particular party member, or a general impression that you recall having about the party at the time. You can tell me anything from that period that you can recall about AD. I'll give you a minute or two to think about it, and then we can go around the table, and I'll ask each of you to tell your story.
3. Now that we have recalled a couple of stories from that time, I'd like to know what you remember thinking about AD, that is, what your opinion of the party was. In other words, at that time in the late 1990s, how would you described AD? Please use the paper and pen in front of you to write down three words or phrases that would have come to mind . . . three words or phrases that best describe what the party meant to you at that time. These can be anything. Once you've written them down, we'll go around the table and everyone can tell us what they wrote.
4. What about COPEI? I'm curious to know how you all would have described the party at that time. What words or phrases would you use to describe that party? As with AD, please write down up to three words or phrases that you might have used about the party in the late 1990s.
5. I'm now going to show you a series of images. I'll ask you to identify the images, if you can, and to share your reactions to these images. What does the image mean to you? What do you think it means for Venezuela? Remember that we don't have to agree about these images and what they mean to us. [In each case, the moderator will first show a picture of the political party's logo, a picture of the political party's founder, and a picture of the most recent president from the party.]
6. (Ranking exercise) As you all know, politics has changed since Hugo Chávez was elected. For one thing, Venezuela has a new constitution. Also, new political parties are competing, and new politicians are being elected into office. Let's talk about these changes. What has changed positively since Chávez was elected in 1998? To answer this question, I'd like us to come up with a list of the three most positive changes that the country has undergone.

Box 3.3 (Cont.)

7. What about negative changes? Can you identify three or more negative changes that the country's political system has undergone?
8. Now I'd like us all to think about AD today. I'd like you to think about what you know or have seen about AD more recently, let's say over the last five years. What do you think about AD today? Has your attitude toward the party changed?
9. What about COPEI? What do you think about COPEI today? Has your attitude toward the party changed?
10. I have one last question for you all. As you know, neither AD nor COPEI has been very successful at fielding presidential candidates over the last ten years. Why do you think this is? Why do you think that Venezuelans stopped voting for the parties? In your opinion, what would each party have to do differently so that people would begin voting for it again? Let's begin first with AD and then consider COPEI.
11. (Final, reflective question) Is there anything else you'd like to mention about either AD or COPEI? Something you'd like to add that hasn't already been mentioned?

what counts as a "good" question grows with one's own experience. In the meantime, you should pre-test your questions with a pilot focus group, whenever possible. You can also share your protocol with colleagues or, even better, friends or contacts living at the research site, to ensure comprehension. And as with all good research, it will be useful to stand on the shoulders of those who have undertaken focus groups previously. Seek out and carefully study the question protocols of those studies you most admire. Ask their authors about any tradeoffs that were undertaken, particularly good choices that they made, or any regrets they might harbor about their question protocol.

Finally, keep in mind that the focus groups themselves will be extremely informative about the quality of the question protocol. With a set of four or five focus groups, you may decide, after carrying out two of them, that a certain question does not work or is not informative. In my case, I quickly discovered that presenting Peruvians with images of former political leaders associated with *fujimorismo* was not particularly illuminating. All participants across the first two focus groups immediately recognized all of them. I promptly decided to leave out that question in order to give more time and space for the questions that were eliciting useful and varied feedback. Certainly, this advice will be less useful when the research design includes only one or two focus groups. Under this circumstance, the objective of the focus group will likely be exploratory in nature. Where this is the case, it makes less sense to ask a set of structured questions, and concerns about the quality of the questions should be mitigated.

Additional Considerations Regarding Non-Native Settings, Sensitive Subjects, and Power Differentials between the Researcher and Focus Group Participants

The information covered in this chapter so far is broadly applicable to the wide diversity of settings where focus groups can take place and to the multiple topics that focus groups may cover. In some circumstances, however, extra care may be required as a part of focus group preparation. The researcher may need additional information to create a data collection setting that is as "natural" as possible for the focus group participants. This is the case, for example, when undertaking focus groups in non-native, or international, settings. It is also true when the subject matter of the research is sensitive in nature. This final section considers the extra work involved in preparing for focus groups in non-native settings and when addressing sensitive subjects. It ends with a brief statement on the power asymmetry that operates between the researcher and focus group participants in all focus group settings.

Focus Groups in International Settings

The primary challenge that researchers will confront when carrying out research in international or cross-cultural settings is that they are outsiders – foreign scholars who, explicitly or not, are relying on the knowledge of natives to enrich their own research. There are at least two consequences to this research asymmetry. First, researchers must undertake additional work to ensure that their focus group preparations are informed by the cultural and linguistic practices of the setting in question. I address these concerns in this section and the next section. Second, the power differential that implicitly exists between the researcher and her research subjects is augmented by cultural differences inherent to undertaking focus groups in a non-native setting. I address this very real and important concern in a separate section.

When carrying out focus groups in a non-native setting, the researcher will often be "unfamiliar with the nuances of language, cultural milieu, and traditions of the study participants" (Hennink 2010, 208). Given this, researchers will likely need to rely on local citizens for help with language considerations, recruitment strategies, and focus group logistics. Recall that the focus group should replicate, to the extent possible, a natural (i.e., non-contrived) setting in which participants will discuss certain questions. This has obvious implications for language. Focus groups should be conducted in a/the language of local participants – that is, a language in which participants feel comfortable speaking. Language choice should be made in consultation with local guides or, in the absence of these, someone familiar with the research site (Hennink 2007).

Language is not just a concern for focus group conversation. It will be vital for recruitment, note-taking, and transcription and translation. Whenever possible, the researcher should strive to preserve cultural nuance and subtle meaning of the context in which the focus groups take place (Hennink 2010, 214). After all, focus groups are meant to give voice to their participants. The implicit value of the data collection method is lessened when that voice is constrained, interrupted, or misunderstood.

The most obvious implication of this is that, whenever possible, the researcher should use native speakers to moderate the focus group, transcribe the conversations, and translate them into the language of the researcher. This adds some costs in terms of time and energy. The researcher will want to budget additional time in her fieldwork schedule to identify and train local assistants for these roles. Depending on her familiarity with the focus group setting, she may need several days or even weeks to identify, recruit, and familiarize local citizens with her project. But these are necessary costs and, whenever possible, should not be avoided.

In some cases, it may not be possible to utilize locals in these positions. The researcher may not have the time or the money to enlist local help. One (suboptimal) alternative is for the researcher to moderate the focus groups. In this case, an interpreter should be hired to maximize comprehension during the focus group. Keep in mind that the in-time translation will necessarily interrupt the flow of the conversations that unfold. For the same reason, the researcher should avoid imposing her own language on the participants. Focus group data are emic in nature. The participants should be allowed to speak as freely as possible. (To be sure, sometimes these suboptimal linguistic choices are necessary. The researcher should make a note of this in her analysis and consider the consequences of these choices on the quality of the data gathered.)

In addition to language, there are undoubtedly cultural considerations that must be addressed when carrying out focus groups in non-native settings. The recruitment process, for example, should be sensitive to existing social structures, local protocols, and norms (Hennink 2010, 216). Recall that recruitment must also correspond with the expectations of the researcher's IRB or ethics committee. In some situations, meeting both of these objectives can be quite difficult. In the best scenario, you can work with your IRB representative to shift their expectations to the exigencies of cultural context.

For example, when undertaking a project to investigate how the Bedouin tribe in Negev, Israel, evaluated its health services, the researchers decided to recruit participants who knew each other, a strategy that required sacrificing anonymity. The researchers noted that their strategy corresponded better with the tightly knit nature of Bedouin tribal society, where interactions tend to be highly regulated and disclosure with strangers highly restricted (Borkan et al. 2000, 209).

Similarly, researchers may find that it is not possible to meet their IRB's preferred method of consent. Often, the written consent of focus group participants is required for the method to be permitted by a local ethics committee. In some cases, however, this kind of consent may be difficult to obtain – for example, in settings where there are high rates of illiteracy or where written consent, as a form of identification, may put participants at risk or make them suspicious of the conversation to follow. Here, researchers should work with their review board to find a more culturally appropriate method of consent. For example, it may be possible to obtain oral consent (Hennink 2007, 37).

Finally, the researcher should be cognizant of any reservations that participants may have with video- or even audiotaping the focus group conversation. In some contexts, the (mis)use of information may be a real concern of the participants. Here, the researcher may decide to forgo recording altogether and simply take notes (Borkan et al. 2000, 209).

It will now seem more than obvious to you that the role of the moderator when undertaking focus groups in non-native settings is more important than ever. In addition to facilitating focus group conversations, this person may serve as cultural translator, local gatekeeper, and logistics manager for the work you wish to carry out. Indeed, as much as you, the researcher, will need to "train" this individual on the nuances of your project, he or she will very likely need to train you on the nuances of local context. In this sense, knowledge will be a two-way street, and your decision with whom to work will be instrumental to the data collection process (Hennink 2010, 212; see also, Hennink 2007, 78). Given the vital importance of this local help, it may make sense to identify and train more than one person to carry out this role. First, this strategy will allow you to choose the best individual to moderate the focus groups. Second, if your first choice falls through, you will have others to call upon. Finally, where resources allow, you may decide to employ more than one individual to help with your focus groups. In addition to a moderator, for example, you might hire a note-taker to be present in the focus groups. You may also want a person for help with transcription and translation (Hennink 2007, 79).

Box 3.4 "Seeking Emirati Women's Voices: The Use of Focus Groups with an Arab Population"

In this study, the authors undertook a series of focus groups involving sixty Emirati women of childbearing age living in the Al Ain District of the United Arab Emirates (UAE). The UAE has a conservative Islamic culture, where most women are confined to their home and are only allowed to leave with a male family escort. With education a growing priority in the country, a large majority of women attend university. As they increasingly enter the workforce, women are beginning to defer marriage and child-bearing to a later age. The study in question sought to identify the health needs of this female demographic, as a way to plan for further services and programs.
(*Source*: Wilkins Winslow et al. 2002, 568–569).

Overall, when undertaking focus groups in non-native settings, researchers should respect and replicate, to the extent possible, the social situation in which participants might typically find themselves. This will likely require additional costs in terms of the time, energy, and resources invested. But the pay-offs will be high, as the researcher can ensure that the data collected is less encumbered by the researcher's own cultural footprint. And, of course, as with all focus group preparations, the researcher should make note of the preferred process through which she would like her non-native focus groups to come together, as well as any and all deviations that occur.

Let's conclude this section with an example of focus group planning, in theory and in practice, in a non-native setting. Wilkins Winslow et al. (2002) undertook a focus group-based study (for context, see Box 3.4) in the UAE. The article considers the host of cultural, gendered, and other concerns that they identified as germane to organizing focus groups with Arab women. First, the authors noted that focus groups were a highly suited data collection method, because it reflected certain patterns of Emirati socialization, including an oral tradition in the country, plus the existence of formal reception or sitting rooms, called *majlis*, where women typically gather (Wilkins Winslow et al. 2002, 568).

Given the restricted freedom of movement of their female participants, the researchers adopted a participant-led recruitment strategy. Specifically, the researchers identified and secured the assistance of three co-workers. These women agreed to bring other eligible family members. They also chose the time and place where the focus groups took place (Wilkins Winslow et al. 2002, 569). Having organized the focus groups to be as sensitive to cultural practices as possible (see, e.g., Wilkins Winslow et al. 2002, 574), the researchers none-theless encountered certain complications in the process of data collection.

For example, the initial site of the focus groups had to be changed. To arrive at the original site, female participants were dependent upon their male family members, who did not prioritize the study. Consequently, later iterations of the focus group were moved to places where women typically (and more easily congregated). A table and chairs were eschewed for sitting on the floor, a common practice in social settings. The researchers found that, while some subjects were addressed easily in the group settings, others, including certain psychological and sexual questions, were not. The researchers decided, consequently, to follow up the focus groups with individual interviews. Finally, the English equivalents for certain Arabic words were difficult to ascertain. The researchers asked for clarifications in meaning during the focus group conversation. They also later worked with an Emirati assistant to help with translation (Wilkins Winslow et al. 2002, 569–573).

In all, the researchers encountered several unexpected complications. Some were easy to address, such as re-modeling the physical space to ensure the comfort of participants. Some required in-time specification, as when the researchers sought to understand the meaning behind a word or phrase. Other complications, however, required significant adaptation, including the identification of a new focus group site that respected the women's restricted freedom of movement. Perhaps most significantly, the researchers decided to adopt a new data collection method – that of individual interviews – to respect perceived discomfort to discuss certain issues in the social setting. The implications of this study for our purposes are twofold. First, when carrying out focus groups in a non-native setting, researchers will need to be sensitive, informed, and also flexible to any complication that occurs. Second, focus groups that address sensitive topics carry their own set of considerations that we should consider now.

Focus Groups and Sensitive Subjects

While Wilkins Winslow et al. (2002) found that some topics were, perhaps, too difficult to address with groups of Emirati women in their project,[4] other researchers (see, e.g., Farquhar and Das 1999; Kitzinger 1994, 112; Liamputtong 2011; Morgan 1996) assert that focus groups are actually particularly well suited for addressing research on sensitive topics. There are reasons for this, as discussed in Chapter 1. Focus groups serve as a setting of

[4] In fact, the decision to use interviews to discuss more difficult or sensitive topics is not without its problems either. Madriz (1997) states that women were actually less likely to discuss sensitive subjects when they sat down individually with the interviewer. This was because the power dynamic between the researcher and her subject was much more evident in a one-on-one, rather than group, setting. More on this in the following section.

mutual support (Kroll et al. 2007, 697). They create “layers of communication” that “provide respondents with a safe environment” to express their ideas (Liamputtong 2011, 110). Overall, the group setting can ease the discomfort of discussing a difficult issue, especially after one person opens the discussion and breaks the proverbial ice on the matter (Barbour 2008, 18).

Of course, for the focus group to be successful in collecting data on a sensitive topic, participants must be willing to speak. Here, the work of the researcher and, again, the moderator is important. Sensitive topics – those that might be “intimate, discreditable or incriminating” in nature (Renzetti and Lee 1993, ix, as taken from Liamputtong 2011, 108) – require special care when considered in any data collection setting. This includes focus groups, as Wellings et al. (2000) duly note. The following are some of the things to keep in mind.

For one, question order matters. The researcher will want to consider how quickly and to what degree a particularly sensitive topic is broached. Wellings et al. (2000) recommend starting with more neutral questions – breaking the ice, as we called it above – before turning to more delicate or difficult subjects. How quickly the focus group turns to these subjects should be gauged by the moderator (Wellings et al. 2000, 257). On this point, careful attention to non-verbal cues of discomfort or reluctance is important.

Additionally, focus group composition can affect openness. Here, what a researcher loses in terms of participant homogeneity (that is, with respect to discord and disagreement) she likely gains in terms of enabling a comfortable space for participants to speak (Wellings et al. 2000, 258). Finally, it should be noted that hesitancy and difficulty in expression are informative for the researcher and can constitute data (Wellings et al. 2000, 259–260). That said, no participant should under any circumstances feel forced to speak against their wishes.

On all these points, the moderator and the researcher are important. The latter must work with her IRB or ethics committee to create a question protocol and plan of action that is thoughtful to the sensitive nature of the research at hand. The former must both manage the focus group neutrally, in the face of uncomfortable and even unpalatable interventions, while also setting the stage for the difficulty of the conversation that follows. For example, the moderator should use language that encourages group openness. One way to do this is for the moderator to share something about herself that reflects her own willingness to be vulnerable. (In fact, having a moderator that matches, to the extent possible, the demographic group of the focus group participants is ideal.) Finally, the moderator should exploit her interpersonal skills, and especially empathy, to monitor levels of discomfort and, where necessary, change the nature of the conversation underway (Wellings et al. 2000, 259–260).

It bears emphasizing, once more, that focus groups are often considered well suited for addressing difficult or sensitive topics. Madriz (1997) makes this point in her own work on the fear of crime in women's lives. She found that many women, and especially Latina women, were more comfortable discussing their own experiences with crime in a group setting, because it was less threatening than other data collection methods, including interviews. Specifically, one woman said to her, "When I am alone with an interviewer, I feel intimidated, scared" (Madriz 1997, 165). Additionally, the group setting allowed Madriz to include undocumented women, because they were not alone in their situation but instead in the company of others (Madriz 1997, 165).

Indeed, Kvale (2006) problematizes the idea that interviews, as a preferred alternative to focus groups for discussing sensitive topics, allow subjects to freely discuss their opinions. That interviews are democratic is a "fantasy"; instead, there is one person who primarily gains from the experience. Therefore, "claims of participation disguise the exertion of power" (Kvale 2006, 482). Interviews are inherently asymmetrical. They are "a one-way dialogue, an instrumental and indirect conversation, where the interviewer upholds a monopoly of interpretation" (Kvale 2006, 484). Focus groups relieve some (but not all [see below]) of these asymmetries by including multiple subjects. It is much more difficult for the researcher to exert control. The power imbalance between researcher and subject is counteracted by the sheer number of subjects involved. If they wish to take the conversation in a particular direction, there is little the researcher can do to stop them.

Overall, while researchers must take special care in organizing focus groups around more sensitive topics, the nature of the research should not dissuade them from using the method. Indeed, for many researchers, it is the social nature of the focus group that makes the method apt for systematically considering these topics. The group setting creates a space for shared experience among participants. Additionally, focus groups defuse, at least partially, the power dynamics between the researcher and her subject(s). That said, it is undoubtedly the case that power dynamics imbue the focus group method, as they do all data collection methods (Hunleth 2011, 82). Before concluding this chapter, therefore, let us briefly consider the power differentials that exist in the focus group setting and which should, consequently, be kept in mind.

The Researcher as "Other": Power Dynamics in the Focus Group Setting

Power exists in all social relationships. This is especially the case in the research setting, where the researcher seeks to benefit unilaterally from the solicitation of specific information from others. In some cases the power differential between the researcher and the subjects is especially apparent. Take, for example, a situation in which a researcher from a developed country is studying topics that affect individuals in the developing world. Or when a white, male researcher wishes to study a topic related to female persons of color. In these situations, for historical, social, and/or contextual reasons, it is often difficult to establish a relationship of equality between the researcher and the research subjects.

Acknowledging this power imbalance is essential for the successful collection and analysis of any data obtained from human subjects. In the focus group setting, the quality of the data is in great part a function of the honesty and engagement of the participants. Focus group data are emic in nature and socially produced. If participants are influenced disproportionately by the researcher's perceived position of authority, rather than by the focus group conversation, then the integrity of the data will be compromised (Stewart and Shamdasani 1990; Krueger 1998a). Put simply, it is not a good thing when focus group participants tell a researcher what they think she wants to hear.

Notably, we lack consensus regarding the nature and impact of the power dynamic between the focus group researcher and her subjects. Some assert it is inherent to the data collection process and can dramatically affect the quality of data collected (Jakobsen 2012). Others, by contrast, say that the dynamic between the researcher and participants can have myriad expressions. A researcher may be "a chair, a safe third party . . ., a witness, an ally, a conduit to a wider audience, and a student in need of instruction" (Ayrton 2018, 13). Moreover, because power is an "inevitable facet of social life," focus group researchers should accept it and attempt to examine its effects (Ayrton 2018, 13). Regardless of one's position about the impact of power, I have yet to see a scholar claim that the researcher-subject(s) relationship is *not* imbued by a power differential.

How, then, can we deal with this power dynamic? There are multiple options. A first step is to create, to the extent possible, a focus group setting that broadly reflects the social experiences that participants live on a daily basis (Vissandjee et al. 2002). This will de-emphasize, if not fully eliminate, the artificial nature of the conversation. Second, the researcher should strive to use a moderator that is as similar to the participants as possible. This makes it more likely that the participants will see the person managing the conversation as an equal. Next, the moderator should be attentive to when/if the participants engage her as an equal. For example, to what extent do they include her in some social norm or a shared understanding (Ayrton 2018, 13)? How often does this occur? In other words, how much of a power differential is actually operating during the conversation?

Finally, the moderator should interject as little as possible, allowing the participants to take control of the conversation. Jakobsen (2012) calls this "decentering," which involves shifting the participants' attention away from the moderator, who she is, and how to relate to her, and toward the other participants and the discussion at hand (Jakobson 2012, 122). She also offers strategies on how to do this. For example, the moderator can ask participants to share their responses to a question with their neighbor prior to voicing it aloud to the entire group. This can complicate attempts to find the "right" answer, while also helping participants commit to a response before sharing it with others (Jakobsen 2012, 122). Alternatively, the moderator can, first, ask a question of the group and then leave the room so that the group discusses the answer without any outside influence (Jakobsen 2012, 124). The moderator would tape the conversation and ask the participants to summarize their discussion upon her return.

Overall, the power differential is a fact of life of the data collection process. As a researcher, your job is to acknowledge it exists, take the steps that you deem necessary to mitigate it, and make note of how it might nonetheless affect the conversation that unfolds.

Conclusion

This chapter has outlined the multiple steps that researchers typically take to prepare for undertaking focus groups. As indicated in Table 3.1, the researcher should ask herself a set of practical questions. The answer to each will help define focus group logistics, the process through which participants will be recruited, consented, and brought together, and the key actors, materials, and objectives of the focus groups themselves. Specific attention was paid to the role of the moderator, who is charged with facilitating the focus group conversation, and the question protocol, which orients the conversation that unfolds. We spent additional time, too, on the extra care that must be taken to prepare for focus groups in non-native settings and when addressing sensitive research topics. In general, we noted that the power imbalance that operates between the researcher and her research subjects should be acknowledged as preparations are made and conversations unfold.

It is now time to consider the focus group itself! At this point, the researcher should be ready to actually carry out the data collection method in the real world. The next chapter outlines some important considerations to bear in mind during the focus group itself. Remember, however, that, with focus groups, as with many (if not all!) data collection methods, much of the hard work has been undertaken well before the focus group ever takes place. On this point, Alexander Graham Bell was correct: "Before anything else, preparation is the key to success."

Exercises

3.1. You hope to carry out focus groups with indigenous communities in sub-Saharan Africa. You wish to understand how the arrival of international non-governmental organization (NGO) workers, who have brought with them new projects designed to more efficiently harvest water, have affected the daily lives and agricultural practices of those communities. In preparation, you have researched different tribal groups and learned that most adhere to fairly strict norms of cultural hierarchy, which make it difficult for women to speak freely in front of men and for younger women to speak freely in front of their elders. Design a series of focus groups that help you answer the research question while being sensitive to these norms. How many focus groups will you undertake? How will they be composed? What can you do to check for the presence of group think?

3.2. You wish to study the dietary practices of undocumented families in low-income urban areas. How would you recruit this group? What strategies might you employ to ensure attendance? What strategies should you keep in mind as you prepare to discuss the day-to-day life of this vulnerable group?

3.3. Regarding the study from Exercise 2.1, provide a description of the ideal moderator for this project. What characteristics are absolutely essential? Why?

3.4. For a project examining the factors that might explain the reduction of racial prejudice in the workplace, you wish to speak with human resources managers about the perceived effect of diversity training. Devise a set of eight to ten questions that help you assess this point. Briefly explain what the objective of each question is with respect to the overall goal of the focus group.

4 Undertaking Focus Groups

The focus group emerged in a rather impromptu way, when Paul Lazarsfeld asked Robert Merton to join him as he monitored individual responses to different radio morale programs. Participants pressed different red or green buttons to reflect their negative or positive responses to different aspects of the programs. Lazarsfeld's assistant then asked a series of follow-up questions. Here is where the story gets interesting. To Merton's dismay, the assistant's questions were not focused enough on specifically expressed reactions. To add to his frustration, Merton felt that the assistant was inadvertently guiding participants to respond in particular ways (Merton 1987, 552–553). In each case, the potential of the focus group for eliciting useful information remained unmet.

Merton's focus then (and, as it happens, my focus now) on these two weaknesses in the follow-up group interview were consequential. Merton's experience with the flawed "focussed [*sic*] interview" provoked him to think more seriously about what a group interview could and should entail. They helped him clarify how focus groups could be undertaken properly. These lessons are useful for us as we think about undertaking focus groups in this chapter.

On the one hand, focus groups should seek to elicit broad but also specific insight into the issues and processes under investigation. These dual objectives – seeking both precise and wide-ranging responses – might seem contradictory at first. In reality, the social nature of the focus group facilitates the fulfillment of both goals. The simultaneous participation of multiple participants enables an extended discussion of a potentially broad range of issues – something that might overly tire a single participant in an individual interview. Nonetheless, the moderator can ask individuals to elaborate on particular responses. By probing in this way, it is possible to achieve a level of specificity on certain points that is similar to that of one-on-one interviews.

To achieve this balance of wide-ranging but nonetheless precise responses requires fairly skillful moderation. This leads to my second point – one that was addressed initially in Chapter 3. The moderator is key to undertaking a successful focus group! In what follows, then, we visit some of the logistical details of undertaking focus groups. Then, we consider the general format and sequencing of a typical focus group and discuss some of the challenges that may arise therein. Finally, we will concentrate on certain moderating tasks that can help facilitate an informative and productive group conversation.

One last point on undertaking focus groups. The content of this chapter is designed to walk you through a typical focus group experience. It provides a template, if you will, of what focus groups tend to look like. That said, you have considerable flexibility in tailoring the 90 to 120 minutes to your needs. Moreover, you may notice that this chapter is, relative to Chapter 3 at least, quite short. This is because the actual implementation of a focus group is fairly straightforward once the steps leading up to it, as identified in Chapter 3, have been fully addressed. Put differently: when the focus group is underway, much of the hard work is behind you. And while you should be attentive to small modifications you may wish to implement in future iterations, you should also listen to and engage with the conversations as they unfold. In other words, enjoy the focus groups!

Setting up the Space

Before your participants arrive, you should set up the space in a way that both assures participant comfort and maximizes the data collection process. Ideally, you can set up the table(s) and chairs so that the participants and the moderator are seated in a circle. At the very least, you should minimize the hierarchical position of the moderator vis-à-vis everyone else in the conversation. It is not ideal, for example, to place the moderator at one end of the table, although this may be unavoidable. By integrating, as best you can, the moderator into the seating arrangement, you convey to the participants that everyone's voice matters equally. The researcher, by contrast, should be seated separately from the main set-up. Again, this distance reflects the passive, observant role the researcher will play as the conversation unfolds.

Refreshments – which often include a beverage or two and a light snack, such as cookies or chips – should be located such that participants can access them at any time during the conversation. Certainly, the shape of the room may mean that these are not immediately within participants' reach. This should not be too much of a disruption, however, especially if the moderator encourages participants to serve themselves early on. At any rate, participants should know that they are welcome to more food and drink as the conversation unfolds. The moderator may simply ask them to be as quiet as possible should they need to move to get them.

Perhaps the most important consideration, in terms of maximizing the data collection process, is the placement of the (audio or video) recording device in the room (Bloor et al. 2001). Quite obviously, the data produced in a focus group will be of little consequence if the researcher cannot access the conversation after the fact. Therefore, the recording device should be placed such that it captures everyone's intervention, regardless of where they sit in the room. The researcher should work with the moderator on this point. They should test sound quality throughout the room before participants arrive.

A lot of the logistics of the focus group itself, including the snacks served and the arrangement of the furniture, should be sensitive to the cultural norms and practices of the research site in question. These sensitivities are key to enabling participant comfort. They also imply additional knowledge on the part of the researcher. They remind us, again, that undertaking focus groups in international contexts often involves some extra research and care.

The Focus Group, from Start to Finish

As we move forward with an overview of a typical focus group sequence, it may be helpful to view actual focus groups as a reference. One good option to explore is Peter Hart's Voices of the Voters project, which is sponsored by the Annenberg Public Policy Center of the University of Pennsylvania. The examples are numerous, and the topics are very interesting.

> The Annenberg Public Policy Center has hosted focus groups with voters from around the United States since 2004. Peter Hart, veteran pollster and expert on public opinion, moderates the focus groups. These conversations are intended to draw insight about presidential candidates, campaigns, and campaign issues from voters from a broad political spectrum. An archive of video recordings is publicly available. These videos are very useful for understanding what a focus group looks like in practice. See www.annenbergpublicpolicycenter.org/events/peter-harts-voices-of-the-voters/ (last accessed July 24, 2018).

We can typically reduce the focus group to a set of five stages: (1) the introduction; (2) the initial question(s); (3) the heart of the focus group, where the most important questions are asked; (4) the wrapping-up stage; and (5) the final stage, where participants are debriefed. Let us briefly address each stage in turn.

Stage 1: The Focus Group Introduction

A lot happens in the introductory stage of the focus groups, although, in practice, this stage passes quite quickly. Here, the moderator must undertake three tasks. Each is fundamental for the conversation that follows.

First, the moderator must *set the right tone* for the conversation that follows. The moderator will welcome the group and invite them to partake in refreshments. While the individuals are settling in, friendliness and openness on the part of both the moderator and the researcher is important. First impressions matter! These initial, friendly interactions demonstrate to individuals that, while they have come to a data collection session, there is an atmosphere of congeniality and informality. I find it useful for the moderator to introduce herself and also the researcher, so that the participants know the moderator is running the show.

Once everyone has been seated, the moderator should provide an overview of the overall research project. Keep in mind that she should convey only very general information about the project. Too much specificity can bias individuals toward answering in a particular way. For example, I recently undertook a set of focus groups in Lima, Peru. My project sought to understand why certain Peruvians strongly oppose a particular political movement in the country, called *fujimorismo* (Cyr and Meléndez 2017). Rather than convey the particular goals of the project, however, my moderator told the participants that I sought to understand how Peruvian activists viewed politics in their country today. The introduction was fairly vague in terms of the project's goals. It was also, however, an accurate, if general, reflection of those goals. The moderator therefore allowed participants the chance to assess whether they would like to participate in the project, without giving away what my specific research goals would be.

Once the tone has been set, the next task for the moderator is to *set the ground rules* for the focus group that will follow. This is where participants learn about what their participation, exactly, entails. For example, the moderator can read the consent form out loud at this point. The consenting process often involves emphasizing several things (although the exact nature of consent is IRB-dependent). Participants may learn that their participation is entirely voluntary (and often anonymous); that there are no right answers; and that their answers will be taped (Finch et al. 2014, 218–219). Participants must knowingly consent to these things, so the moderator should be firm on these points.

To be sure, the moderator should also convey these ground rules in a friendly way, in the hopes of reducing the "evaluation apprehension" of the participants (Fern 2001). When ensuring confidentiality, for example, the moderator can assure participants that their words will only appear anonymously in publications. She can emphasize that all data generated will be stored in a password- or lock-protected space. The moderator may offer to take questions at this point, further allaying any potential participant concern. Once participants feel fully informed, the moderator will ask them to sign the consent form. This is also a good time to ask participants to fill out a socio-demographic questionnaire, if the researcher has provided one. Recall that this questionnaire helps a researcher assess the diversity of the focus group and any potential sampling biases that might exist (Bloor et al. 2001, 40).[1]

Finally, the moderator must work to *set the participants at ease*. Participants must feel comfortable in the focus group setting before the questions begin. This is especially important if the focus group will broach some sensitive or difficult topics. The moderator may, therefore, acknowledge the potentially difficult nature of the conversation that will unfold. In so doing, she can suggest that the sensitive nature of the topic is precisely why we need focus groups. They provide key insight on hard-to-address themes (Stewart et al. 2007, Chapter 5).

This is also a moment in which the moderator can disclose some information about herself. Let us take, for example, a focus group in which participants will be asked to share their opinions about a recent election. The moderator may reveal, for example, that she enjoys discussing politics with others and therefore is especially looking forward to their conversation. This helps place the moderator on a more equal footing with the participants. It also helps establish rapport (Fern 2001). In all, the introductory stage is a key moment in which the moderator can create "an atmosphere of trust and openness" with participants (Stewart et al. 2007, 94).

Stage 2: The Initial Question(s)

Once the rules have been established and participants have signed the consent form, it is time to begin. The first question is largely introductory in nature. Each participant should be asked to give their first name and to answer a simple question that is related to the topic at hand. For example, if the overall focus group is about religion and politics, the moderator may ask each participant to talk briefly about the regularity of their religious practice.

The principle goals at this point are twofold. First, the moderator and the researcher will want to take note of each person's name, so that they can track the order of the conversation as it unfolds. Second, this initial question is meant to break the ice. It represents each participant's first intervention in the focus group. It should be simple and fairly straightforward, so as to ease

[1] Depending on the design of the focus groups, a researcher may wish to present the questionnaire at the *end* of the conversation. This can be useful, for example, in certain experimental settings. I find, however, that if the questionnaire only provides socio-demographic information, it is best to have participants fill it out first. This prevents fatigue from setting in, potentially affecting the accuracy of the form. It also ensures that all participants respond to the form. Sometimes individuals are up and out the door before they can be fully debriefed!

each individual into the conversation and warm them up for the remaining questions.

An alternative to the icebreaker question is to present the participants with a focusing exercise (Bloor et al. 2001, 42–47). Focusing exercises are intended to help participants concentrate on the general topic of the focus group – they help "focus" the conversation, as the name suggests. It can involve ranking a set of topics. In this case, the moderator provides a set of statements to the group and asks them to agree on a ranking in order of importance. The moderator may also present a hypothetical case or scenario to the group that is suggestive of some real life situation related to the research topics of interest. Participants, in this "vignette" focusing exercise, are then asked to comment on a course of action to follow. The moderator may also present the group with a photo or image and ask them to describe what they think is going on. Returning to the *Talking Politics* example from Chapter 3 (Gamson 1992), Gamson presented focus group participants with editorial cartoons related to the news topics that they were discussing and asked them for interpretations of and reactions to them (see Gamson 1992, 202–212).

Note that focusing exercises are tasks rather than questions. Unlike a straightforward question, they can, in some cases, encourage participants to work together toward a joint goal from the very beginning of the focus group. While this can be very useful, it may nonetheless be difficult to devise an ice-breaking exercise that is appropriate for the topic at hand. Also, participants may be reluctant to jump right into a group task, especially if they do not know each other. On this point, keep in mind that focusing exercises can also be useful later on in the focus group, as a way to break up the monotony of conventional questions. It can also be a useful tool for asking a particularly important question in a different way, allowing it to serve as a check on validity.

Finally, the moderator should encourage everyone to speak during this first stage of the focus group. It will be increasingly difficult for timid participants to contribute as the conversation deepens. By involving each participant early on, there is a greater chance that they will stay involved throughout the conversation (Finch et al. 2014, 220).

Stage 3: The Heart of the Focus Group

After the introductory question, the moderator should present a set of questions that brings participants into the heart of the research goals at hand. On this point, sequencing is important, as we already emphasized in Chapter 3. For one, each question should, where possible, lead into the next, so that the flow of the conversation is maintained. Where this is not possible, the researcher and moderator should work together to devise an appropriate transition between two unrelated topics.

Moreover, it is often the case that one or two questions are really central to the overall objectives of the focus group. The placement of these should be considered carefully. The researcher will want to maximize group rapport. She will also, however, want these questions addressed before participant fatigue sets in. It may be best, therefore, to place these questions fourth, fifth, or sixth in order (out of, say, seven or eight questions).

The moderator is responsible for moving the group from question to question and for probing particular responses as needed (more on this below). She should do so, however, without overly structuring the conversation (Hennink 2007, 172–176). Ultimately the moderator cannot force participants to address any question directly. Indeed, *how* participants answer a particular question is informative in and of itself. Do they understand what is being asked? Does the question have resonance? In fact, in a set of multiple focus groups, researchers can use the first one or two to adjust or adapt questions in accordance to the quality of the response.

Finally, it may at times be necessary for the moderator to explore diverging views. Sometimes participants appear to come to agreement about a question relatively quickly. To probe this apparent consensus further, the moderator may ask, "Does anyone have a different perspective on this point?" Where conversations are disjointed, the moderator can ask if anyone would like to build off of a point made by somebody else (Hennink 2007, 183). The moderator must therefore strike a balance between allowing the conversation to unfold organically and probing for additional or more precise responses. I return to this point in greater detail at the end of the chapter.

Stage 4: Wrapping Up

The focus group should come to a close with a final question. Often, this entails allowing participants the opportunity to raise an additional point or two that they feel still needs to be addressed. The moderator should signal that this is the final question (Finch et al. 2014, 221). Indeed, she may also indicate that the focus group is near coming to an end in the *penultimate* question (see, e.g., Appendix 1 for an example). It is often helpful to provide these guideposts to participants along the way.

Stage 5: The Debrief

Finally, before participants leave, the moderator should thank each of them for their time. She can also remind them that the researcher is available for additional questions or comments. The researcher, for her part, should be prepared to provide her contact information or her business card. She may also need to field specific inquiries by the participants as they prepare to leave (Bloor et al. 2001).

During this final, debriefing stage, it is often helpful to mention the future direction of the project. This can include the project's next steps, the kinds of outputs that the project will produce, and when these might be available. This is also the time to pass out compensation to each participant. If the benefit of participation is not immediate, the researcher should use this time to inform the participants about how their time will be rewarded.

The Role of the Researcher

The moderator is tasked with much of the work during the focus group. This does not mean, however, that the researcher can sit back on her laurels! Instead, the researcher is often a present, if passive, observer of the conversation. She has one primary role before and after the focus group, and a different role as the discussion unfolds.

First and foremost, the researcher's presence lends credibility to the focus group. She is the project's primary representative. As such, she should be prepared to answer any questions the participants have, both before and after the focus group takes place. I recommend that the researcher arrive with business cards or, at the very least, be ready to provide participants with an email address. Participants often wish to follow up the conversation or follow the project itself as it unfolds.

During the focus group, the researcher should be actively taking notes. This means tracking what the participants say. It is particularly helpful to follow the sequence of interventions. That way, the researcher can avoid the misidentification of participants during the transcription process later on. When I observe focus groups, therefore, I pay close attention to who is speaking to carefully capture the order. I will also, often, directly quote something that each participant says during a particular intervention, so that the transcriber can be sure that the overall intervention is properly attributed.

Beyond this attention to the order of participant interventions, I often try to capture what I think are important insights that each person says during the focus group. This can be quite tiring and, when taken to the extreme, can involve writing down – to the extent possible – as much as possible of what each person says. While this kind of intensive note-taking is not necessary, it will also help with the transcription process. The researcher can also review these notes immediately following the focus group (and before, for example, the written transcript is ready) as a way to draw some initial conclusions about the data collected.

Confronting Certain Challenges as the Focus Group Unfolds

The emic, organic nature of focus groups means that certain human dynamics may affect how the conversation evolves. The moderator and the researcher should be prepared to address these challenges, should they manifest. It is often necessary to discuss them in the pre-focus group encounter between the moderator and the researcher. Especially when the moderator is less experienced, it will be useful for her to have some guidelines regarding how to deal with each (see Table 4.1).

Perhaps one of the most widely discussed challenges that can manifest in a focus group is the phenomenon of **group think.**[2] Group think occurs when a focus group conversation yields consensus, whether or not one truly exists (Copsey 2008). In this case, the social dynamics of the group induce pressures for dissenting participants to muffle their disagreement. Therefore, the data

Table 4.1 Addressing Problematic Social Dynamics in the Focus Group Setting

Dynamic	Why Problematic	Potential Solution
Group think	May reflect false consensus	Ask for written before spoken responses; probe for dissenting ideas
Passivity	Less data collected	Indirect: Eye contact Direct: Invite the participant to intervene
Dominance	Over-representation of one perspective	Indirect: Turn toward someone else; avoid eye contact Direct: Invite others to speak
Hostility	Creates stressful environment	Indirect: Turn toward someone else; avoid eye contact Direct: Invite the participant to take a break or leave
Group silence	Foments discomfort, loss of data	Ask additional, more specific questions; provide examples of potential responses; employ a focusing exercise
Losing focus	Can denote misuse of time	Revisit the original question; turn to the next question

[2] We also briefly addressed this challenge in Chapter 2.

collected by the researcher is inaccurate, since it does not reflect the true sentiments of the group.

Group think can be a problem for focus groups, certainly. Some researchers suggest, however, that, since group think is a dynamic that occurs in our day-to-day social interactions, it actually adds a layer of validity to the focus group process (Hollander 2004, 607). After all, people regularly feel pressure to conform in group settings (Krueger 1994, 10–11). Setting aside the reality of group think, it is nonetheless possible to check for its presence in the focus group setting. Participants can be asked, for example, to write down their responses before voicing them to the group at large (Albrecht et al. 1993, 56–57). This way, the researcher can verify whether what individuals say in the social setting of the focus group conforms with what they initially write. These social forces might also be attenuated by bringing together participants from similar backgrounds.

In addition to group think, a focus group may include an incredibly timid or quiet participant. Here, **passivity** is a concern. When certain participants are overly reticent, then the researcher can lose access to potentially very useful data. After all, passive participants talk less. This means less information is gathered, which is not ideal. Passive participants can sometimes be engaged indirectly. A moderator can invite someone to speak by simply making eye contact. Where this does not work, she can be attentive to potential non-verbal reactions from the participant. If that person nods or shakes her head in response to something, then that can be an invitation for the moderator to intervene and ask her to speak up. Keep in mind, however, that consented participation in the focus group is often predicated on the premise that no one has to speak if they do not wish to. Therefore, the moderator can only do so much with a quiet participant.

Dominant participants, by contrast, are more problematic. They can make it more difficult for others to speak, truncating the data collected in a different way than with passive participants. As a louder and more frequent voice, a dominant person can hijack the conversation and impose her perspective, leaving little room for others to interject. A researcher will want to address (and mitigate) this challenge when it occurs. The moderator has indirect and direct tools for dealing with dominance. Sometimes, a moderator can avoid making contact and even turn physically to face someone else, as if to non-verbally communicate that it is someone else's turn to talk. Where this does not work, it may be necessary for the moderator to invite someone else to speak (Finch et al. 2014, 225). Where even this does not work, the moderator may need to take extreme measures and (gently) cut the person off (Stewart et al. 2007, Chapter 5).

Very rarely, one may encounter an openly hostile participant in a focus group. Perhaps a participant has had an usually bad day. Perhaps she is hostile in her general temperament. **Hostility** occurs when a person is openly confrontational in her actions. Quite obviously, this situation will be extremely disruptive for the group dynamic and will cause a stressful, unenjoyable environment for everyone involved. Sometimes, the moderator can successfully turn the conversation away from the hostile participant by avoiding contact or turning to someone else. If, however, the hostility becomes untenable, then the moderator may have to (gently) pull the person aside and ask her to take a minute to calm down or simply to leave (Stewart et al. 2007, Chapter 5).

There are two, group-level dynamics that may also have to be addressed to preserve the integrity of the focus group. The first occurs when a group, as a whole, does not speak as openly or as freely as one would hope. Sometimes a group may not respond to a particular question. **Group silence** (Hollander 2004; Bloor et al. 2001) can signal that a question is not particularly relevant or properly understood. In the latter case, the moderator may wish to re-phrase the question – often in a way that has been discussed with the researcher when going over the protocol together. Silence, however, when a question has been appropriately interpreted is, by contrast, potentially quite informative. It can signal that the group has little to say on the subject. For example, I undertook focus groups to learn about the stereotypes that citizens associated with different political parties in Peru, Bolivia, and Venezuela (Cyr 2017b). In some cases, the participants had little to say about a party. This silence was quite informative. It suggested that the party had little resonance in society, since citizens could not meaningfully talk about it.

Much more problematic, however, for the focus group are generalized silences. It is every researcher's fear that individuals will simply choose not to speak (Bloor et al. 2001). I have *never* encountered this problem; however, one can imagine that something about a group dynamic might make individuals reluctant to speak. In this case, empathy can go a long way. The moderator can offer up her own answer to the question, as a way to build a rapport with the group and encourage others to speak. (Care must be taken, however, not to *lead* the group by biasing them toward one response.) She can also employ a focusing exercise (see Stage 2 above), which can encourage the group to work together before asking individuals to share their own feelings on a particular topic (Bloor et al. 2001, 52).

Finally, sometimes a group can get caught up in a tangent, pulling the conversation away from the topic of interest and into drastically different thematic terrain (Hennink 2007, 189). These kinds of divergences can be informative. After all, there is a reason that the conversation diverged as it did. When a group **loses focus** and cannot seem to return to the original topic at hand, however, the moderator should be instructed to interject and set the conversation back on course. She can do so by revisiting the question,[3] or, alternatively, by turning to the next question on the list.

The Importance of the Moderator, Revisited

Throughout this chapter, we have seen how the moderator plays a crucial role in: setting the ground rules, establishing an environment of ease, addressing problematic participants, and keeping the conversation on track. We must, therefore, return to a theme from Chapter 3: The role of the moderator is key! Here, I consider the moderator's overall approach to the focus group and, specifically, the careful balancing act that moderating can imply.

When facilitating a focus group, moderators must work to walk the fine line between different attitudinal and behavioral extremes. For example, the moderator will want to project a certain air of authority, so that she can credibly interject into the focus group as needed. Yet, too much scriptedness or formality can make participants suspicious or ill at ease (Puchta and Potter 2004). Similarly, the moderator should not be a predominant figure in the conversations that unfold. Yet, she may have to interject at times, either to elicit a more complete response or to address a particularly challenging participant (see Table 4.1). It is therefore necessary to maintain a careful balance between involvement and passivity. As Bloor et al. (2001) remind us, the moderator is a "background . . ., not a foreground figure" (Bloor et al. 2001, 49), and yet she clearly must also facilitate the conversation to keep it flowing.

On this point, a bit of guidance from the researcher can help. She can (and should!) consider every question on the protocol with the moderator, so that the latter is fully aware of the purpose of each. A question may, for example, have the goal of encouraging a group to consider the different (and potentially conflicting) priorities that might drive vote choices. The moderator can work to draw out these priorities and the tensions between them if the participants do not immediately address the point. Knowing when to probe, in other words, can help a moderator attain the proper balance between intervening and standing off. Probes are ultimately very useful under certain circumstances: (1) to ascertain the specific meaning behind an overly general intervention; (2) to obtain a more complete response; (3) to encourage others to participate (e.g., "Does anyone else have the same reaction as Linda on this point?"); and (4) to seek out dissent (e.g., "Does anyone have a different perspective from

[3] If the group ventures once again down the tangential path, even after the moderator re-emphasizes the original question, then the researcher may conclude that the apparent divergence is not, actually a divergence. Instead, it is a reflection of something meaningful to the topic at hand.

that of Linda?") (Stewart et al. 2007, Chapter 5). The researcher can work with the moderator so that the latter understands the extent to which each probing goal is a priority and for which questions, in particular, probing might be necessary. Appendix 1 provides an example of a focus group protocol that includes moderator instructions that address some of these concerns.

Finally, the moderator is tasked with ensuring that all of the questions are addressed. This will be especially important when the researcher intends to compare across multiple focus groups (Morgan 1996, 142). This may require achieving a balance between probing individuals (or the group) on certain questions that are of utmost importance to the researcher. It will also require, however, the equally important skill of time management. The moderator must regularly check a clock to ensure that the time allotted to certain questions – especially those that engender healthy debate or enthusiasm – does not leave the group rushing to finish at the end. Focus groups should not last more than one-and-a-half or two hours. The researcher can work with the moderator to establish a rough estimate of the time that should be devoted to each question. Knowledge about the relative importance of different questions will be helpful here. Beyond this, however, the moderator should have a sense of when the conversation around a certain topic has been exhausted so that she can move on to the next question. Keep in mind, too, that time management is hardest early on (Stewart et al. 2007, Chapter 5), when the questions tend to be more general and the responses of individuals more tentative, slow to emerge, and, in some cases, even long-winded.

Conclusion

This chapter has addressed the different stages that typically constitute a focus group, from the early introductory phase to the final, debriefing stage. It has identified certain challenges that the focus group setting can provoke, especially with respect to individual and group responses to the questions that are asked. While the researcher has an important role to play in both observing the focus group and taking notes as it unfolds, the chapter has also suggested, in line with Chapter 3, that the moderator is a key player in producing a successful conversation.

To be sure, there is very little that the researcher can do once the focus group is underway. Preparation (e.g., of the moderator, of the question protocol, of the space) is fundamentally important precisely because the researcher's control over what happens in the focus group itself is minimal. As a final note, then, I would encourage the researcher to be constantly attentive to how participants respond to certain questions and the general reactions to the protocol overall. Does the focus group appear to be eliciting the desired information? If so, then excellent! If not, then changes may need to be made before the second, third, or fourth focus group takes place. In the meantime, have fun! Listen to what the participants have to say, and enjoy the fruits of your (preparatory) labor. Hard work – in the form of data analysis (see the next chapter) – is soon to come, and so the researcher should sit back and appreciate the focus group as it unfolds.

Exercises

4.1. Devise two focusing exercises that might be appropriate for an exploratory focus group that wishes to explore strategies for reducing racial prejudice in the workplace.

4.2. Imagine you are undertaking a set of focus groups in a university classroom. The study examines the difficulties of attaining work-study balance among working, first-year college students. How, exactly, would you set up the classroom space to accommodate eight participants, the moderator, and the researcher? What details would you need to keep in mind?

4.3. Access one of the focus group question protocols that is of most interest to you at the Qualitative Data Repository (QDR, https://qdr.syr.edu/ [last accessed July 24, 2018]). Examine the protocol and read the brief project description that accompanies it. Once you understand what the goals of the project are, consider how you would train a moderator to carry out this protocol with a set of focus groups. What specific instructions, if any, would you give to a moderator regarding each question? Which questions would you suggest are the most important? Finally, how would you advise them to address problematic participants? Using the protocol as your guide, write up a set of instructions for your moderator.

5 Analyzing Focus Groups and Presenting the Results

Analysis of focus group data involves bringing order to the data collected, and it can be a process that is ambiguous, time consuming and creative.

(Doody et al. 2013, 266)

A running theme of the book thus far has been that the motivations and objectives of the focus group study should define the choices you make as a researcher. They should guide: where, when, and with whom you undertake the focus groups; the questions you ask; how you instruct the moderator; and whether it will be necessary to refine certain questions in-between focus group sessions. The research question should define your data collection.[1] Let this be a mantra you carry with you always. Given its importance, it should come as no surprise that the research question, and the goals and motivations therein, will largely define how you analyze the data collected. It will also define how you present your findings.

This chapter orients you toward these two tasks. First, it provides some guidelines on how to analyze your data. Rather than putting forth a preferred method of analysis (there are, in fact, multiple methods), this chapter will shed light on the primary issues you must consider as you begin to analyze your own data. Data analysis requires quite a bit of time and creativity, as the quote above indicates. It need not, however, be ambiguous in its execution. The primary objective of this chapter is to explain how you can be *systematic* with your data analysis.

Given the multiple choices you have when it comes to data analysis, it does not make sense to limit your options by emphasizing here one analytical approach over another. Still, this chapter will describe the most commonly used analytical method, if only briefly, so that you have a sense of what analysis

[1] Some authors recommend using one's methodological strengths to guide one's research agenda (see, e.g., Ahmed and Sil 2012). Even here, however, the relationship between methodological choices and research questions remains strong. One would not ask a question oriented toward statistical analysis if one's methodological expertise sat squarely in the qualitative realm. The kinds of questions we ask define the methodological choices we make. The inverse is also true: Our methodological preferences shape and indeed constrain the kinds of questions we might ask (see, e.g., Goertz and Mahoney 2012).

can look like. It will also explain how and when to focus your analytical lens on the three different levels of data that focus groups generate.

Finally, as a last step in your focus group journey, you must think about how to present your findings and analysis to your audience of choice. This can be a client or a group of academic peers. While our focus here will be on presenting focus group data in a peer-reviewed publication, the chapter will provide additional sources on how to present to other types of audiences.

Transcribing your Data

Before we can analyze or present our data, we must first have more tangible access to it. We must, in other words, *transcribe* the data, so that we can see the words on a written page. Transcription facilitates data analysis, because we can actually see the data we wish to analyze. It also makes analysis more rigorous and, therefore, reliable (Krueger and Casey 2015, 19). While often seen as a time-consuming and laborious process, the advantages of transcription far outweigh its disadvantages.

For one, in addition to facilitating data analysis, a transcription represents a written record of the discussion. This can be useful for you as a future reference. Where appropriate, it can also be shared with others (Stewart et al. 2007, 110). When the researcher does the transcribing,[2] she can become really familiar with the data. She can also identify any moderation techniques that she might wish to refine for future focus group iterations (Krueger and Casey 2015, 20).

Transcription may seem straightforward: One simply types what one hears on the recording. At the most basic level, this does sum up the act of transcribing. Still, one should keep a few points in mind – points that will help the researcher organize and systematize the data, such that the subsequent analysis is much easier (see Table 5.1).

For one, you should adopt a consistent transcription style, both within each focus group and across focus groups. Make note, at the beginning of each transcription, of the date, time, and place where the focus group took place. List the number of participants and, where applicable, the socio-demographic features that seem pertinent (e.g. numbers of males versus females). Note the name of everyone in the room.

Clearly delineate the section dedicated to each question. Separate each intervention with a paragraph break. Identify each intervention by name.

[2] It is not uncommon for the researcher to hire someone else to transcribe the focus group conversations. This can be a major time- and energy-saver. Once completed, the researcher will want to carefully review the transcription for accuracy and consistency. She will also probably wish to read the transcription through at least once before beginning to analyze the data therein.

Table 5.1 Tips for Transcribing

1. Be consistent
2. Type interventions word for word
3. Take note of special sounds (e.g., sighs, snorts, laughs)
4. Include non-verbal communication
5. Make note of context
6. Allow for sufficient time
7. Use playback equipment, if available

Source: Adapted from Krueger and Casey 2015, 20.

Finally, type each intervention in its entirety. This may seem superfluous – especially as time passes and it feels like you are advancing ever so slowly in your transcription. It may be tempting to only transcribe those interventions that seem salient to the question at hand (Ruthmann 2008, 47). I caution against this approach, however. If you limit what you transcribe, then you limit the data to which you have access moving forward. Especially early on in the research project, you may not know what information is more or less salient. Finally, by only transcribing what seems salient, you potentially bias yourself against considering alternative hypotheses or explanations. For all of these reasons, I recommend forging ahead with an entire, word-for-word transcription. The hard work is worth it.

Be sure to note sighs, snorts, laughters, shouting, or especially loud (or soft) interventions, when they occur. This can be done quite simply by bracketing the action when it occurs in the text. These special sounds will be important for interpreting the meaning behind someone's words – something that is much more difficult to do once those words are transcribed and the recording is set aside.

Indeed, the transcription should also reference non-verbal communication. This, as with the special sounds that may accompany certain interventions, is crucial for understanding meaning and context. Does the participant roll her eyes when she speaks? Does she look down, as if embarrassed? Certainly, in noting non-verbal communication, one introduces a certain amount of subjectivity into the transcription process. Still, these non-verbal cues convey additional information and should be noted whenever possible. (Note, too, that an audio recording will *not* capture non-verbal forms of communication. This is where extensive note-taking during the focus group will be particularly consequential.)

Overall, the transcription must be attentive to context, nuance, and communicative subtleties. The tone and emphasis with which one speaks is as informative as the words themselves. As Stewart et al. (2007) point out (p. 111), the phrase, "that is bad," can actually mean that something is good. Moreover, the meaning of a sentence changes depending upon which word is emphasized. Take, for example, the comment, "This was good" (Krueger 1998b, 33):

1. This was GOOD. (Inferred meaning: It was good.)
2. THIS was good. (Inferred meaning: This one was good, but others were not.)
3. This WAS good. (Inferred meaning: It used to be good, but not anymore.)

Table 5.2 provides an example of how these non-verbal cues can be transcribed for subsequent ease of understanding and interpretation. The excerpts come from focus groups on pregnancy after perinatal loss and on AIDS/HIV prevention in women (Morrison-Beedy et al. 2001, 52).

The first column provides the exact quote. The second column includes additional notes that come from the researchers' comments and from the tape recording. Finally, we see how the text appears in the actual transcript, including the additional data in parentheses and the authors' added notes in brackets. This third column reproduces excerpts from a systematic transcription. One can read the transcript and understand, first, what was said; second, what additional non-verbal or verbal cues were conveyed; and, third, what the researchers' own interpretations were.

Of course, this kind of transcription work takes time and effort. The researcher will be integrating data from multiple sources (i.e., the recording, the notes, and real-time interpretation). Achieving this much specificity may not be necessary for an entire conversation. Still, where non-verbal cues or other contextual or interpretative information seems pertinent, it may be useful to add them in. I find it useful to consider what it might be like for me to read the transcription six months after the focus groups take place. What information will I need to have to reliably come to the same conclusions about a particular phrase or intervention? If something beyond the words themselves seems useful in facilitating that recall process, then I include it from the beginning.

Finally, technological advances are such that it is increasingly financially feasible to obtain playback equipment that will make transcribing considerably less painless. You may have access to a "transcription kit" with a foot pedal that allows you to control playback speed and frees up your hands for typing (Krueger and Casey 2015, 20). In the absence of a foot pedal, audio player software, such as Express Scribe, facilitates the playback process with the keyboard itself. A program such as Dragon, by contrast, transcribes text recited into the software for you. Here, you should be prepared to check for any errors that might occur in the recitation.

Table 5.2 Integrating Relevant Data into a Transcript

Exact quote on transcript	Additional data (source)	Completed transcript
"It was no big deal."	Eyes looking downward (field notes); Sarcastic delivery (tape).	"It was no big deal." (Said sarcastically, with eyes looking downward.) [It really was a very big deal to her but others had not acknowledged that.]
"I am monogamous. I only have sex with other guys when my man is in jail. If he gets out, I only have sex with him."	All of the other women in the group were shaking their heads, in agreement (field notes). "Am" was said with emphasis (tape).	"I am monogamous! I only have sex with other guys when my man is in jail. If he gets out, I only have sex with him." (The other women agreed with her definition of monogamy by shaking their heads.) [The researchers' first impression was that the participants didn't understand the definition of monogamous, we then realized that the participants had a shared meaning that differed from the research teams'.]
"I told myself, I will have a baby."	Leaning forward, pounding fist on the table, near tears (field notes); stated with conviction, emphasis on "will" (tape).	"I told myself (pause), I will have a baby!" (Her whole body was part of the statement, leaning forward, pounded fist on table when she said, "will" and on the verge of crying). [Trying to have a baby was a driving force in her life, she wasn't going to give up without a baby. It was a painful memory].

Source: Morrison-Beedy et al. 2001, 52 (Table 2).

Analyzing your Data

Now that you have a transcript, it is time to dive into the words on the page and analyze their content. Recall that your data analysis should be driven by the motivations and objectives of the focus group. On this point, it pays to keep a few things in mind. Are you simply triangulating data generated via a different method, in an effort to corroborate those finding? Alternatively, do the focus groups comprise the primary data collection methods? In the latter case, you will likely want to devote considerable time and energy to categorizing, summarizing, and interpreting the results. With the former, your analysis need not be quite so profound.[3] Summarizing general sentiments expressed in the focus group, and selecting a few quotes that are broadly reflective of those sentiments, may be sufficient (see Posner 2005 for an example).[4]

For most of you, however, a more in-depth approach to analysis will be necessary. Multiple options exist in terms of *how* to analyze your data. I describe one of these in detail below and reference others for your potential interest. Most analyses of focus group data involve analyzing the content of the conversations that took place. Data analysis is, in essence, content analysis. Therefore, whatever analytical approach you adopt, one major goal will be to craft a systematic and comprehensive overview of the data (Wilkinson 2016, 84). In many cases, analysis will also involve interpreting the data, or attempting to capture the meaning participants attach to different ideas or concepts.

In what follows, I first provide a checklist of the kinds of factors you will want to keep in mind as you analyze and potentially interpret data content. I introduce this checklist first, because how you approach analysis in many ways is more important than the actual type of analysis you undertake. To some, content analysis might seem ad hoc, subjective, and just plain "soft" (Krueger 1998b, 67). Of course, many more know this is not true. Still, as with all data analysis, certain general guidelines are useful to keep in mind as you analyze focus group content. You should strive to be systematic in your analysis and to consider all sources of information. You will want to exercise caution when interpreting data and embrace complexity. You will also want to be attentive to issues of reliability and validity (Kidd and Parshall 2000, 302–303).

[3] Unless, of course, your focus group findings refute the data collected elsewhere. In this case, you may need to revisit your initial conclusions and develop a strategy moving forward regarding how to deal with contradictory evidence (see, e.g., Seawright 2016).

[4] Of course, as I suggested in Chapters 1 and 2, using focus groups simply to triangulate results garnered elsewhere is not the best or most efficient use of the method. It is, however, the most common (Cyr 2016).

One last thing before we explore the set of factors to keep in mind: Timing is always a consideration when analyzing focus group data. Specifically, the sooner you can begin to analyze your data, the better off you (and your analysis!) will be. You want to keep the focus group conversation fresh in your mind as you begin to ponder what kind of data it generated. This might mean simply reviewing your notes in the immediate aftermath of the focus group and jotting down your initial hunches, interpretations, and ideas (Krueger and Casey 2015, 21). A first stab at summarizing the data is an early attempt at analysis. Once you write down these initial musings, you can revisit them, along with the transcript itself, as you begin to analyze the data more systematically. They will help you "return" once more to the focus group setting where the data collection took place.

Factors to Keep in Mind when Analyzing Focus Group Data

When you undertake data analysis, you will likely want to pay attention to several things. Some of these are fairly general in nature. Some are based on the data. As discussed above, focus groups produce information that is both verbal and non-verbal. I therefore consider factors related to each type of information.

General Factors to Keep in Mind

Be systematic. When it comes to focus group data analysis, you should strive to be as systematic as possible. What do I mean by systematic? The analysis you undertake should be well-documented, self-explanatory, and, consequently, easy to articulate (Krueger and Casey 2000, 128). This might mean coding the units of data (be they words, phrases, or full participant interventions) by a well-defined set of rules, using colors, symbols, or notes. Systematization will allow you to fracture the data into parts and reassemble it in new ways (Krueger 1998b, 11). It will facilitate analysis *across* focus groups. It will also enable others to help you with analysis or to undertake their own analysis later on.

Perhaps the easiest way to be systematic is to write down the rules by which your analysis takes place. Where your analytical choices are made explicit, then you maximize the likelihood that the analysis, overall, is reliable. This means that your content analysis would produce similar results across time or across multiple coders or analysts. You can achieve, in other words, internal consistency (Kidd and Parshall 2000, 302–303). Moreover, while replication is not necessarily a goal of qualitative researchers, it is important to be able to effectively communicate the analytical choices you make to others.

Overall, there are at least three reasons why you should strive to be systematic with your data analysis. First, it will make the analysis of multiple focus groups (and potential future iterations of the project) more homogenous. Second, it will be easier to present your data when the time comes (more on this below). Finally, you will have the tools to answer any questions that might emerge about *how* you came to your conclusions in the first place.

Focus on patterns. Content analysis involves identifying patterns in the data. Do similar themes emerge across multiple questions? Do they emerge across different focus groups? Recognizing these trends and tropes is a big part of analyzing focus group data. The kinds of patterns that emerge will depend on the purpose of the study (Krueger and Casey 2000, 140). Before analysis begins, the researcher should have a sense of what she is looking for, thanks to the goals of the project and existing research.

Be open to multiple interpretations. While you may have a sense of the kinds of data your focus groups will generate, you should *not* enter the data analysis stage looking for any specific pattern in particular. As you will see, focus groups generate A LOT of data. Analyzing it may seem, at first, quite daunting. Finding any patterns at all may seem difficult. Be prepared, therefore, to embrace the complexity that awaits you (Barbour 2008). Be open to multiple interpretations. I raise this point not only to prepare you for the potential stress of focus group data analysis. You must also be open to the possibility that your intuitions about what is going on are wrong. Your analysis should be open to alternative explanations. It should seek to explain divergent patterns both within and across focus groups (Krueger 1998b, 15).

Retain a healthy skepticism. Many scholars caution against taking participants' words at face value, especially when it comes to group agreement. They suggest that what looks like consensus can instead be a reflection of group dynamics and pressures (Sim 1998, 348). In earlier chapters, we considered the effects of the group dynamic on individual interventions. While I think it is possible to assess consensus at the group level (more on this below), I also think it is important for researchers to maintain a healthy skepticism when it comes to analyzing a focus group transcript. Do individuals seem unusually flexible in their statements? Does an intervention reflect group tendencies, even if it directly contradicts something that person said earlier? On the other hand, does agreement on a particular point or question come, perhaps, too quickly? Researchers can leverage past experience with focus groups, or compare dynamics across a set of focus groups, to help address these questions.

Table 5.3 Verbal and Non-verbal Factors to Incorporate into Your Analysis

Verbal Factors	Non-verbal Factors
Words Used	Context
Frequency	Intensity of expression
Extensiveness	Issue absence
Specificity	Time spent on any one issue
Internal consistency	

Verbal Factors to Keep in Mind[5]

Words used. Most principally, you will want to take careful note of the words and phrases used to answer questions and describe phenomena. Specifically, you might want to ask: What meaning do participants attach to those words? As Table 5.2 indicated, in a study of pregnancy after perinatal loss and on AIDS/HIV prevention in women (Morrison-Beedy et al. 2001, 52), the researchers and the participants had a different understanding of the term, monogamy. You will also want to assess the variety of words used to describe a phenomenon or answer a question. Do participants use the same words? Is this true within and across focus groups?

Frequency. Frequency refers to the number of times a topic, word, or phrase was used in a focus group. Was one word or phrase particularly predominant in the discussion of a question? Did it appear several times in one focus group? In multiple focus groups? Frequency can help you assess how important a word or phrase was for understanding or describing a phenomenon.

Extensiveness. Extensiveness refers to the number of participants who used a particular word or phrase. The researcher might wish to know how often a word was mentioned (frequency). She might also wish to know how widespread its use was (extensiveness). She may wish to specifically quantify extensiveness (e.g., 73 percent of all participants believed the advertisement was too complicated). The researcher could also speak in more general terms (e.g., a large majority of the participants believed the advertisement was too complicated). Like frequency, extensiveness is an indication of the weight or importance a word or phrase has for a set of participants.

Specificity. The researcher will want to note how specific participants are in their responses. Were responses to a particular question vague? Did a probe

[5] See Table 5.3. The primary source for these verbal factors is Krueger and Casey 2015, 22. Additional sources are referenced explicitly in the text.

add additional detail? Did participants speak in the first or third person? In considering these questions, a researcher can assess the sense to which participants were confident in their answers or, indeed, took ownership of them. For example, the statement, "I believe monogamy is important because it demonstrates loyalty," indicates a greater sense of opinion ownership than the statement: "Our society values monogamy." In the latter case, the individual asserts what she thinks that *society*, and not necessarily she, believes.

Internal consistency. Here, the researcher will want to assess how consistent participants are in their responses. Do they respond similarly to a question as the conversation unfolds? What about across different questions? Was the shift in opinion abrupt? If so, then the researcher may be more skeptical of the participant's interventions. If the shift followed the flow of a conversation, however, then it may be that the answer is complex or nuanced. It will also be useful to see if the participants themselves (or, indeed, the moderator) noted the shift in opinion and how that shift was addressed.

Non-verbal Factors to Keep in Mind[6]

Context. When it comes to focus groups, context matters. No statement should be taken out of the context in which it is embedded. Is the conversation heated? Is one person dominant while others are merely reactive in their interventions? Is reference to other events or past conversations important? Is there a particular tone, such as sarcasm, that must be noted to interpret appropriately what someone has said? (These kinds of notes should be incorporated into the transcript; see the section on transcripts above.)

When it comes to context you should also consider what is happening, not just in the focus group setting, but outside it as well. Are political, social, or environmental events underway that might affect the overall tenor of the conversation (Krueger 1998b, 34)? For example, if the focus group asks questions that are political in nature (i.e., about political parties or government), it might matter if it takes place between election cycles or during campaign season. In the latter case, political issues may be highly salient. Consequently, individual opinions may be more passionate or intense than they otherwise might be.

Intensity of expression. Indeed, the intensity with which participants discuss different topics should also be noted (Stewart et al. 2007, 115). Are participants duly responding to questions but not particularly engaged in the conversation as it unfolds? By contrast, are they really passionate and even acting out their

[6] See Table 5.3.

comments? Do they raise their voice? Gesture with their hands emphatically? Does their speech quicken? These cues – especially when they differ from the overall tenor of the conversation – can indicate that participants are placing special emphasis or weight on a particular point or question.

Issue absence. Certainly, the researcher should pay close attention to what is said in the focus group setting. It is also important, however, to take note of what is not said (Barbour 2008; Stewart et al. 2007, 114). For example, a researcher may be struck that, in a conversation about what makes a successful social policy, the issue of cost does not arise. Ideally, a researcher or moderator will have caught this omission in real time and will ask why it was not raised. Where that does not occur, these omissions can be "tricky" to analyze (Krueger 1998b, 37). It can mean that the issue was not as important as other issues that participants raised. Still, you cannot know for sure. However, these omissions become increasingly important theoretically when they occur in multiple, and not just one, focus groups.

Time spent on issue. Finally, if participants spend more time on some questions versus others, then it can be an indication of how important those questions are to the participants. If a question is addressed methodically and quickly by only a handful of participants, then this is, in and of itself, informative for the researcher. Perhaps the question was not properly understood. In this case, the question may need to be refined or re-worded. Alternatively, the question may not be relevant for the participants. Equally informative are those questions that receive a lot of attention – especially when they generate a lot of discussion. These are probably more germane or relevant to the group (Stewart et al. 2007, 115), and the researcher should take note of this.

Classic Content Analysis: The Most Common Analytical Approach

The most common approach to analyzing focus groups is with classic content analysis, which is also known as the scissor-and-sort or cut-and-paste technique (Krueger and Casey 2000, 136–138; Stewart et al. 2007; Onwuegbuzie et al. 2009; Doody et al. 2013; Wilkinson 2016).[7] This kind of content analysis can occur by hand – literally, with scissors and a lot of table space – or with the use of a computer. (Analysis may also involve computer software, a point I revisit a bit later in this section.) Either way, the primary objective is to code and categorize the data so that the researcher can convey the general themes, trends, and patterns that emerged within and across focus groups.

[7] Other approaches to focus group data analysis include keywords-in-context, discourse analysis, and micro-interlocutor analysis (see, e.g., Onwuegbuzie et al. 2009; Doody et al. 2013).

How, then, to undertake this kind of content analysis? First and foremost, you (the researcher) should read the transcript carefully. As you read, you should begin to take note of certain patterns that emerge. Do participants answer questions in the same way? Do some questions evoke more debate than others? Do certain words or phrases appear multiple times when discussing a phenomenon or event? Even at this early stage of analysis, you will want to keep the factors we reviewed above in mind. It would also be useful at this point to review any initial impressions or musings about the focus group(s) that you wrote down immediately following their execution. This way, you can re-familiarize yourself with the text before you begin the coding process.

Having re-immersed yourself in the transcript(s), you must now begin to code the conversations. To do this, you can proceed question by question, taking note of the different interventions made by participants. You will want to code words, phrases, entire interventions, or some combination of these[8] according to the unique themes or descriptors that emerge. Take note, as you go, of the logic by which you establish different categories. For example, you might work inductively, creating categories as a function of the interventions themselves. You may also have considered an initial (but not exhaustive) set of potential categories from a review of the relevant literature. Either way, to be as systematic as possible, you should be explicit about these choices.

As you code and categorize you will want to devise a system by which you separate different themes. You can choose to color code different interventions. You might also copy and paste them into a new document separated into categories or themes. (In fact, the original name for this analytical process, called the scissor-and-sort approach, was due to the practice of literally cutting texts from a hard copy of the transcript and sorting them into groups on a long table [Krueger and Casey 2000, 132].) Note that this coding and categorization process is highly iterative and not necessarily linear. You may add new categories, group previously formed ones, or eliminate others altogether as you read and re-read the transcript. The process is also highly inductive and comparative: New pieces of information are compared with the text already sorted and categorized (Krueger and Casey 2015, 25). It will be helpful to maintain a clean copy of the transcript handy, so that you can examine the sorted and re-assembled text alongside the original conversation to ensure, for example, that context is not lost.

[8] Some authors (e.g., Wilkinson 2016) recommend choosing a unit of analysis (i.e., a word, phrase, or intervention) at which to code. This may be appropriate for certain studies, and it may, in fact, be required by a software program should you use one to do the coding and classification for you. However, I find it useful to be more open in terms of how you unitize. It may be useful, for example, to place certain individual words and phrases into the same category if they reflect a similar sentiment or idea.

When the coding and classification is complete, you should have a list of themes and/or categories associated with each question or each concept/phenomenon of interest. At this point, you may wish to ask one or two others to re-code the transcript to check for reliability. You may ask them to undergo the same process that you carried out, to see if they come up with similar themes/categories. This can be a big ask, however, as it will take time. You might also simply provide them with the (non-filled) list of themes/categories that you constructed and ask them to fill it in with the words, phrases, or interventions that they feel best belong with each theme. In the latter case, you can at least confirm the reliability of the groupings within the major, identified themes (Stewart et al. 2007, 116–117).

If you and your fellow coders do not agree on certain themes or certain categorization schemas, then you will have to work together to decide how best to deal with those disagreements. Perhaps a more general category works. Perhaps two categories need to be aggregated or combined in different ways. Once you have reached an agreement, however, you will have successfully re-ordered the text to reflect the patterns that emerged in the conversation.

At this point, you can begin to analyze and interpret the patterns. You may want to identify representative quotations of a particular theme or category. You can also, where appropriate, quantify the number of responses associated with each theme or category as a way to adjudicate the weight of different responses to a question or phenomenon (Doody et al. 2013, 266). Keep in mind, again, the list of verbal and non-verbal factors we mentioned previously as you work to connect the patterns and categories back to the broader research questions that defined your study (see Table 5.3). Note, too, that the frequency and extensiveness of a particular word or phrase will convey different information than *how* something was said and situated within a particular conversation (Wilkinson 2016, 86). Both types of information can be useful, depending upon the goals of the overall study.

In fact, where you place your analytical focus will depend largely on what you hope to accomplish with the focus group data. For example, it might make sense to focus more on individual interventions than on exchanges between different participants. Alternatively, you may be interested in group dynamics, especially whether there is consensus on different topics. In the next section, I explain when and how one might analyze data specifically at the individual, group, or interactive level.

Before we turn to the different levels of analysis, however, I will conclude this section with two final points. The first may seem obvious: The classic content analysis explained here is easiest to manage with a computer (rather than with scissors, paper, and a long table). In fact, different software programs exist that can perform a lot of the content analysis for the researcher (although the software is by no means necessary). In Appendix 2, I have provided a brief summary of five of the most commonly used computer software packages that can help with the analysis of focus group data, along with a set of references where you can find more information on the computer resources available.

Please note that the different software programs can help make your data analysis more systematic (Krueger 1998b, 91). They are not as helpful, however, when it comes to capturing and interpreting non-verbal cues or context. Still, when dealing with an unusually large number of focus groups, the help of NVivo or something similar can be vital. In a study on family caregivers of individuals with Alzheimer's disease, David Morgan undertook thirty-five focus groups. The data likely amounted to hundreds of pages of transcripts! Here, the computer was "a powerful indexing and cross-referencing tool" (Krueger 1998b, 89). Still, while the computer did some of the work, Morgan and his fellow researchers nonetheless undertook the heavy lifting of establishing the categories and the coding. Ultimately, whether and how much you rely upon a software program depends upon your research goals and your familiarity with the program itself. Once more, please see Appendix 2 for some initial guidance on the packages that are available.

Finally, in an effort to remain as systematic as possible with your data analysis – whatever approach you choose – you may find it helpful to establish a set of instructions regarding how you coded and classified your data and which verbal and non-verbal factors you took into account as you analyzed and interpreted the results (Stewart et al. 2007, 123). These instructions will be extremely useful for presenting your data. They will also be helpful should you rely upon others to help you code. Additionally, the list of instructions will be crucial should you decide to replicate the project (and, consequently, the data analysis) in the future.

Distinguishing the Individual, Group, and Interactive Level of Analysis

In Chapter 1, we noted that one unique feature of the focus group is that it produces data at three different levels of analysis: the individual, group, and interactive levels. When a researcher focuses on the individual level of analysis, she examines the specific interventions that different participants make, without much regard for how those interventions follow in sequence or comprise an exchange of ideas.

The group level of analysis, by contrast, centers on the conversation as a whole. How do the participants address a particular topic or question, and where does the conversation take them? When focusing on the group level of analysis, a researcher will follow the group as it discusses the ins and outs of a particular topic. She will pay special attention to where the conversation ends: Is there consensus? Did the group divide over the issue? Did the group veer far off track and end up discussing something else? What meaning did they assign to the topic at hand?

Finally, at the interactive level of analysis, the researcher is most interested in the conversational journey. She will focus on specific exchanges that reveal nuance, contention, and deliberation. While the end result may also be of interest, a focus on the interactive level of analysis means that the researcher wants to capture the messiness of social dialogue. Perhaps a surprising nugget of information will be revealed – a tangent from the main conversation that provokes a new hypothesis or idea. Perhaps the researcher simply wants to understand the process, that is, *how* a group works through the discussion of an idea or topic.

Each level of analysis, as suggested above, produces different kinds of data. Yet, researchers have typically struggled to acknowledge these differences. And, in fact, several scholars (Carey and Smith 1994; Kitzinger 1995; Duggleby 2005) lament that focus group researchers tend to privilege the individual level of analysis. They note that, generally speaking, we lack "guidance" on how to incorporate the impact of group context into our data analysis (Carey and Smith 1994, 123). In the worst-case scenario, the data analysis will ignore the social context altogether, such that one struggles "to believe that there was ever more than one person in the room" (Kitzinger 1995, 104).

In this section, I rely on previous work (Cyr 2016) to provide at least some guidance on how to incorporate different levels of analysis when analyzing focus group data. I show that, while a researcher is welcome and in fact encouraged to examine data at all three levels of analysis, she may nonetheless choose to focus her analytical lens on one level. This is defensible, I suggest, because each level of analysis helps a researcher meet a distinct research goal (see Table 5.4). It is therefore possible to align the purpose of the focus group with the overall research design, the objective of the focus group data, and the level of analysis under investigation. While the goals identified in Table 5.4 are not exhaustive in nature, they do reflect how focus groups are most typically used in the social sciences (Cyr 2016). Depending on the goal, then, a researcher can place her analytical focus on the appropriate level of analysis for the task at hand.

The Individual Level of Analysis

A focus on the individual level of analysis has generated some controversy (see, e.g., footnote 8 from Chapter 1). But it is the most widely leveraged level of

Table 5.4 Combining Research Goals and Level of Analysis

Purpose of focus group in the research design	Objective of the focus group data	Level of analysis
Triangulation: To produce data intended to corroborate evidence collected via other methods	*Economy of scale*: To rapidly appraise multiple individual opinions simultaneously	*Individual*: Emphasis on the words, phrases, and interventions of single participants
Large-N Pre-test: To produce data intended to evaluate the content of a large-N instrument	*Measurement validity*: To craft context-specific questions for a survey or experiment	*Group*: Emphasis on the end result of a group discussion
Exploration: To produce initial data on a topic about which we know very little	*Hypothesis-building*: To develop arguments to explain a phenomena/issue	*Interactive*: Emphasis on specific exchanges, nuance, and the topics explored as conversations unfold

Source: Modified from Cyr 2016, Table 2.

analysis of focus group-based research, both in marketing and in the social sciences (Cyr 2016, endnote 14). At this level of analysis, the researcher is curious to know what different individuals think about, or how they react to, the particular phenomenon under investigation. The researcher will likely ask, "What does an individual think about X? Do others agree? If so, how many?"

Typically, when researchers focus on this level of analysis, they are leveraging focus groups for the economies of scale they provide (see Table 5.4). A focus group allows a researcher to gauge multiple individual opinions and reactions simultaneously. Rather than interview ten people individually – a task that can take hours – a focus group enables one to reach all ten people at once and in under two hours. In terms of time, the focus group can be quite efficient.

A review of studies that focus their analytical attention on the individual level of analysis reveals that the large majority used them to confirm evidence acquired via other data collection methods. In other words, the purpose of the focus groups was triangulation. Here, the efficiency of the economy-of-scale approach to the focus group is particularly appealing. One need only organize one or two focus groups to confirm what the researcher has already learned from other methods.

Data collected at the individual level of analysis is particularly amenable to a quantitative approach to content analysis. The researcher can count the number of times each individual or multiple individuals used a descriptor to characterize an event, person, or phenomenon. She can also create a database or grid of the individual-level responses, to ensure ease of comparison across individuals, subgroups, etc. (Barbour 2008). A simple word count can indicate with precision the percentage of individuals who, for example, responded positively or negatively to a particular product or issue.

Again, many scholars (Carey and Smith 1994; Kidd and Parshall 2000; Sim 1998) find data produced at the individual level to be less trustworthy. For them, the group dynamics inherently affect how individuals react. Consequently, one cannot know for sure that what an individual says in the group setting reflects what she might say on her own. To ignore the group setting, they argue, is tantamount to incompletely or inappropriately analyzing the data (Carey and Smith 1994, 125).

It is possible, however, to mitigate the effects of the group dynamics on the individual. For example, in my work on party brands in Latin America (Cyr 2017a), I wanted to understand how each group of participants spoke about different political parties. I was primarily interested in the *group* level of analysis. Still, I thought it might also be useful to survey how each individual described each party. Therefore, I asked them to write down a few words or phrases to describe the party before discussing it as a group. In so doing, I could reasonably assume that these answers were free from any social pressures that emerged during the discussion of their responses. I used these individual-level, written responses to construct a database of descriptors for each party.

Table 5.5 provides an example of how this kind of database might look, relying on hypothetical reactions to a campaign advertisement as content. The database is organized into several columns, dividing the data by focus group number, participant, sex, overall response to the advertisement, and, finally, the written responses each individual used to describe the advertisement. While this kind of quantitative classification of data is not necessary, it can facilitate an analysis of the frequency and extensiveness of the descriptors used.

To analyze these data, one might wish simply to add up the positive versus negative reactions and provide a percentage of each. One could also group together those descriptors that reflect similar sentiments. "Cheesy," for example, does not reflect the same sentiment as "vulgar," although both might be considered negative when it comes to assessing reactions to an advertisement. When deciding whether and how to aggregate terms, it is useful to return to the objectives of the study. Because she is studying reactions to a particular campaign advertisement, the researcher in our hypothetical example might want to group together words that are positive (e.g., hopeful, optimistic, confident), those that are fairly neutral (e.g., unremarkable), and two sets of negative terms. For example, "cheesy" and "cheap" are certainly negative. But the terms "vulgar," "offensive," and "tasteless" – words that indicate moral reprobation – are arguably much more problematic for a person seeking to attract votes. Citizens who think an advertisement is cheesy might nonetheless be willing to vote for the candidate. Someone who finds the advertisement offensive or vulgar, however, might be more averse to the candidate after seeing it.

In this case, then, the researcher will likely want to report the frequency and extensiveness with which each term (or group of terms) was used. How many people found the advertisement to be "vulgar"? Was this a widespread sentiment? If so, the campaign may choose not to use the advertisement. How the analysis unfolds, in other words, depends largely on the goals of the project overall.

The Group Level of Analysis

Ideally, the researcher in the advertisement example used immediately above (see Table 5.5) will have instructed the moderator to probe the particularly egregious responses to the advertisement. That way, she could have a sense of why certain individuals reacted so negatively. The probe might also spark a general conversation within the focus group about whether others had a similar reaction while watching the advertisement, however fleeting. Overall, by getting the group to speak with each other about the advertisement, the researchers could have a sense of how they, as a whole, reacted to it and if they reached consensus in terms of its impact. Here, the focus would shift from the individual to the *group* level of analysis.

For some projects, the group will be the primary focus of the analysis. As stated above, when a researcher focuses on the group level of analysis, she is interested in what the group, as a whole, has to say about a topic or question. She may ask, "How closely did the group adhere to the questions? Were related issues brought up? If so, how? When? What were the contradictions that emerged? How did the group resolve disagreements? Did they? Did any topics produce consensus?" (Duggleby 2005, 834). Ultimately, a researcher can use the focus group to gauge the extent of shared meaning or understanding around a topic. She can also summarize a conversation about the topic, assessing where the participants ended up as a group.

Given their social nature, focus groups are particularly good at capturing the group level of analysis. They can gauge how groups think or interpret certain ideas or concepts. This task – that of assigning or interpreting

Table 5.5 A Database of Individual-Level Data

Focus group	Participant	Male	Positive reaction to the ad?	Words used to describe ad . . .	
1	A	Y	Y	Optimistic	*n/a*
1	B			Cheesy	Overblown
1	C		Y	Hopeful	Optimistic
1	D	Y	Y	Confident	Hopeful
1	E	Y		Cheesy	*n/a*
1	F			Tasteless	Vulgar
2	A	Y	Y	Confident	n/a
2	B	Y	Y	Promising	Positive
2	C	Y	Y	Assuring	Optimistic
2	D		Y	Hopeful	n/a
2	E			Cheap	Unremarkable
2	F			Terrible	Offensive
2	G			*No response*	*n/a*
3 . . .	A . . .	Y . . .	Y . . .	Promising	Hopeful

Note: This table is in reaction to a (hypothetical) campaign ad that might be shown in a focus group setting. The response, n/a, indicates that the participant did not put forth a second word to describe the ad. "No response" indicates that the participant preferred not to offer a response.

meaning – means that the group level of analysis is particularly useful for researchers who use focus groups as a pre-test for some sort of large-N project (most typically a survey but also, potentially, an experiment).[9] The group can help a researcher to elaborate questions for a survey or to confirm that a question (or model or game) has been appropriately worded or phrased. The group can also help a researcher understand how a question may have to be asked differently. In all, the focus group becomes an important pre-test for measurement validity (Adcock and Collier 2001; see also the earlier discussion on measurement validity from Chapter 1 of this book).

When analyzing group-based data, the researcher tends to focus on how much consensus exists around a topic or question. Do the participants interpret a question in the same way? Do they speak about a topic using similar terms? The answers to these questions will either help to confirm or refine a proposed protocol for a large-N study. That way, the researcher can feel sure

[9] Of course, using focus groups as a pre-test for a large-N study is not the sole reason one might undertake focus groups and analyze the data produced at the group level. Still, it is by far the most common reason that social science researchers analyze group-level data (Cyr 2016).

that the survey or experimental instrument tapped into appropriate, contextually sensitive language, tone, and/or sentiments (Table 5.4).

Group-level data help, then, to gauge the level of consensus in a focus group. Assessing agreement (or lack thereof) often means paying close attention to how a conversation ends. Recall that, generally speaking, opinion formation typically occurs in social settings (Hollander 2004, 607). This process is decidedly non-linear and potentially contentious. To ask if a group arrives at consensus, therefore, means to see how the group ultimately concludes the discussion (Cyr 2016, 243).

To be sure, the researcher should be careful to assume that easy agreement on an issue means, in fact, that consensus truly exists. We considered this problem earlier in the chapter. Group dynamics may mean that more timid participants are uninterested in pushing back against a particularly dominant viewpoint (Duggleby 2005, 834). The moderator will be crucial here. She can specifically look for alternative opinions or push apparently skeptical participants to voice their opinion. By alerting the moderator to these potential challenges, and by paying close attention yourself, you can gauge the extent to which a consensus is false (Onwuegbuzie et al. 2009, 8). As we already emphasized, a healthy dose of skepticism goes a long way to helping one analyze data.

The Interactive Level of Analysis

Focus group conversations about a topic or question can be quite lengthy. This means that, in addition to assessing whether consensus was achieved, potentially a lot of data will be produced as individuals talk to each other. Certain exchanges, as I suggested above, may be contradictory, puzzling, or entirely surprising. Others may reflect your (theoretically derived) expectations. Whatever the case, these exchanges are informative. They also involve analyzing data at the *interactive* level of analysis.

The interactive level is the least exploited in focus group-based research (Kitzinger 1995). Often, it is treated as a part of group-level dynamics (see, e.g., Duggleby 2005). This certainly makes sense. Interactions involve more than one person. They are inherently social. Still, I believe it is useful to distinguish the group from the interactive level of analysis. Measuring how a group comes to an opinion (or opinions) on a question is very different from assessing the process through which that opinion was forged. The information gleaned, consequently, is different.

At the level of interactions, a researcher will want to ask the following questions: What are the points of inflection, reflection, or interest? Does debate occur? Was the discussion particularly heated, tense, or emotional? Which statements evoked conflict? Did any alliances form among group members? Was any new or unexpected information produced (Duggleby 2005, 834)? In other words, were there surprising moments? Were those moments fleeting, or did participants spend time discussing something unexpected?

A focus on the interaction is particularly useful when one knows very little about a topic or question. Focus groups can allow a researcher to explore a new question or develop possible explanations for a question. When these are the goals of the focus groups, the researcher will want to pay close attention to the exchanges that take place (Table 5.4; Cyr 2016, 248). Certainly, this will not be the *only* level of analysis appropriate for this research purpose. The group level of analysis will also likely be useful. Still, the multiple exchanges that take place will help a researcher assess how much debate there is and how many different explanations or reactions a question produces. For exploratory projects, a researcher will want to explore all possible explanations, not just the predominant one.

How, then, to analyze the interactive level? When focus groups are undertaken for exploratory purposes, a "simple descriptive narrative is . . . appropriate and often all that is necessary" (Stewart et al. 2007, 109). In-depth analysis of the transcripts, be it quantitative or qualitative in nature, will be less useful because the conclusions drawn will be highly tentative. A researcher will instead simply want to report what is said. She will convey the general tenor of the discussion and, certainly, the different reactions that the discussion produced. She may wish to reproduce, as qualitative evidence, those exchanges that were particularly illuminating or surprising. When the focus groups are organized for exploratory purposes, the researcher will, more than anything, seek to obtain a lay of the land. She will develop hypotheses to be explored subsequently, either through a new set of focus groups or with a different data collection method.

Focus groups produce data at different levels of analysis. This can represent an analytical challenge for the researcher. This section has suggested that there are some shortcuts that one can take if it is not feasible to examine and report data at all three levels of analysis. The purpose of the focus groups for the research design, together with the particular objectives of the data they produce, can help you concentrate your analytical gaze on one or another level of analysis. The individual level of analysis is quite informative for the purpose of triangulation. The group level of analysis is helpful when assessing the measurement validity of a large-N instrument. The interactive level of analysis is useful for exploratory work and for crafting new hypotheses.

Presenting your Data

Once you have analyzed your data and gleaned a set of findings, you must prepare them for presentation. This is the last major step in your focus group journey. Congratulations on making it here! Now, depending on *where* you must present your data, you face one last challenge: Making all the appropriate information fit. As we will see, this is really only difficult when the space that you have is limited. If you are writing your results for a stand-alone report, then you probably have an unrestricted amount of space and can worry less about what (not) to include – although, certainly, your audience will undoubtedly reward brevity! The same is likely true for a book-length manuscript, where you have the liberty to create an appendix for most non-vital information.

The challenge of presenting focus group data is much greater for peer-reviewed articles in social science journals – articles that are often restricted to 12,000, 10,000 or even 8,000 words in length. In this medium, the researcher will likely not have the luxury to print the entire question protocol or provide a full rendering of the content analysis undertaken. Certainly, appendices, online or otherwise, are increasingly common even for article-based research. This is a great relief for focus group researchers and for qualitative researchers more generally.

Still, the questions of *what* to present and *how* to present it remains. In a peer-reviewed article, answering these questions properly is crucial for transmitting credibility, for the purposes of reliability, and for convincing your peers that, in fact, the study is worthy of publication. Space is even more tightly restricted in a mixed-methods research design, where focus groups are one of multiple methods that have to be addressed within the word limit.

So, what to do? This last section is divided into two parts. The first provides a set of guidelines for presenting focus group results in an article-length setting. The second considers how to present focus group-based work in a medium that is much less restricted in length, specifically, for stand-alone reports or book manuscripts.

Before we briefly examine both approaches, a word on overall style is in order. Although the amount of space can shape what, exactly, you present to your audience, you must always be concerned about *how* you present your findings. Quite obviously, you want to be engaging. This will mean writing with a style that is amenable to the medium of choice, certainly. It also requires being concise and to the point. Avoid the use of jargon. Where possible, use examples from the transcripts. Overall, know that this kind of writing requires time and effort (Krueger and Casey 2000, 149). But the added investment in style will undoubtedly help with your work's impact.

Presenting your Data . . . when Space is Tight

In a previous work (Cyr 2016), I noted that few norms exist regarding how to present focus group-based data in an article-length format. This conclusion was based off of a meta-analysis of published studies that used focus groups in their research design. That analysis revealed that the kind of information published about focus groups was highly variable. In many cases, even the most basic concerns were left unaddressed, including the kinds of questions asked and the number of focus groups carried out. I therefore created a set of three guidelines that I suggested were sufficiently informative and yet succinct enough to fit into a restricted, article-length space (Cyr 2016, 250–251).

First, make explicit the main purpose of the focus groups for the research design. Were they pre-tests for a different data collection method? Were they meant to produce triangulating evidence? Whatever the purpose, it should be clearly stated. The justification for using focus groups, and not some other method, to achieve that purpose should also briefly be addressed.

Second, note the level of analysis (individual, group, interactive) that will be the focus of your analytical attention. In most cases, the level of analysis will make sense given the main purpose of the focus groups (as per Table 5.4). Where this is not the case, you should defend why the level you are analyzing is the most appropriate for the task at hand.

Finally, list the exact phrasing of those questions that were cited directly in the analysis section. In the best-case scenario, *all* questions will be included (perhaps in an online appendix). But when pressed for space, you should, at a minimum, provide the precise language of the specific questions to which you directly refer in the text. You should also footnote the number of participants across the full (specified) number of focus groups you carried out.

These three pieces of information represent an absolute minimum when it comes to presenting your work. While not fully informative in terms of the focus groups you carried out, it will allow a reader to: understand why you used focus groups in the research design; assess your analytical focus; and know, at the very least, what specific questions were asked that informed the overall conclusions. Additional data, including the full question protocol, the recruitment strategy, and the precise analytical approach undertaken, can and, where possible, *should* be included in an appendix, online or otherwise.

At a minimum, you should offer to make this information available upon request.

Presenting your Data . . . when Space is (Relatively) Unrestricted

In this scenario, you will have to worry much less about what you present, because you will have more space to work with. Of course, the stylistic concerns mentioned above still apply, so please keep these in mind. Potentially unlimited space does not translate into unlimited patience or time on the part of your readers.

If the final presentation is a stand-alone report, then it will look slightly different than if you were to incorporate your findings into a larger book manuscript. Stand-alone reports, or narratives (Krueger 1998b), will often be oriented toward audiences that have specifically requested the focus groups be undertaken. These are fairly conventional and have a template that you can follow.[10] Nonetheless, much of the content will be quite similar to that of the book manuscript, even if where it appears in the text differs.

In what follows, I include a basic overview of the information that should appear about the focus group in either written medium (see also Krueger and Casey 2000, 149). Where you choose to put the information will depend on the overall organization of the publication.

First, you will want to include a summary of the most pertinent information about the focus groups (this would be an executive summary in the stand-alone report). Here, the information will look very similar to that which would appear in an article-length text (see the previous section). Specifically, you want to explain why the focus groups were undertaken, that is, what their purpose was for the larger research project. You also want to explain your objectives for the data collected. Here, you should see some alignment, as per Table 5.4 and our discussion above. The purposes of the focus group should match with the kind of data collected and analyzed.

You will also want to provide the questions that specifically informed the analysis undertaken. The full set of questions will be included elsewhere – and most likely in an attached appendix. You do not, however, want to make the reader look elsewhere to find the exact phrasing of the questions that were the most consequential for your analysis. Finally, you want to include the number of focus groups that were organized and the number of participants involved in each.

To be sure, you will want to include a complete description of the procedures undertaken to make the focus groups happen. In the book manuscript,

[10] See Krueger (1998b, 109–114) if you wish to follow this template faithfully.

Box 5.1 Creating an Appendix on Focus Group Procedures

The following is a list of those items that it can be helpful to include in an appendix to a book manuscript (or, alternatively, in a section on focus group procedures in a stand-alone report).

- Number of focus groups, when and where they took place;
- Average duration of each focus group;
- The compensation provided;
- A description of who the moderator(s) was (were);
- A description of the researcher's role (if she was not the moderator);
- A table of descriptive data, including, for example, pertinent socio-demographic information about the participants (e.g., percentage who were women, average age, average education);
- A description and justification of the recruitment process, as well as requisites for participation;
- A copy of the socio-demographic questionnaire if you used one;
- A copy of the full question protocol;
- A description of any pertinent instructions given to the instructor;
- A description of the data analysis, including, where applicable, the coding procedures at the different levels of analysis leveraged and any database that was created of the data generated;
- Any limitations that you encountered as you carried out the data collection method, what you did (if anything) to mitigate those limitations, and how they might affect the overall findings.

these will often occur in an appendix. For an example, see Appendix B in Cyr 2017a (219–230). The appendix includes potentially a lot of information (see Box 5.1). My goal was to be as transparent as possible with the process. I sought to convey the logic behind my methodological choices and the limitations I faced as I collected the focus group data. In providing this level of detail, I allow others to assess the merit of my findings based, in part, on the choices I made in collecting data. Where possible, this kind of data transparency is, I believe, valuable for the knowledge-building enterprise.[11]

You will have to include a description and analysis of the major findings from the focus group work undertaken. These should focus on the overall goals

[11] Note that I do *not* provide the transcripts of the focus groups themselves. I am not advocating that any researcher do this, certainly. Should you be interested in making these data available, data repositories, such as the QDR at Syracuse University, exist that know how properly to archive transcripts and administer them to other individuals.

of the project. If the goal of the focus groups was triangulation, this section will explain if the focus groups corroborated other data and how. If the purpose was to pre-test a survey or experimental protocol, then the results should focus on what the pre-test revealed and those changes, if any, that were undertaken as a consequence of the focus groups. The inclusion of a few examples will be helpful in either case.

Finally, it may be appropriate to set aside space to interpret the findings. What did the focus group data reveal that you did not otherwise know? What can you glean from those revelations? Do they suggest new avenues for research? Do they provide nuance about other theories or other gaps in the literature? This section is optional, and some of it may actually be better placed in the results/analysis section. Still, for larger projects – and especially for exploratory work – it may be useful to spend time on the broader implications that the focus group data raise.

Ultimately, the presentation of focus group data will be a function of the demands of the project, the expectations of the audience, and/or the particular norms of the social science discipline in question. This section has outlined, broadly and briefly, the main components that should be included when presenting your focus group work. Still, for more specific guidance, it will be useful to study how others have presented their work in a medium similar to that in which you hope to publish. The expectations in sociology may differ, ultimately, to those of political science or geography. Seeing how others have published focus group data will be immensely helpful as your prepare to publish yours.

Conclusion

This chapter has outlined several considerations that you should make as you analyze your focus group data and present your findings. Rather than adopt a prescriptive approach and explain how, exactly, content analysis should occur, it provided a series of recommendations to contemplate as you carry out the analysis from start to finish. First, it suggested being as specific (and systematic) as possible with transcription. When you maximize the amount of information translated to the written page, you make data analysis more accurate, reliable, and valid.

Second, it highlighted a set of factors that you should keep in mind as you begin your data analysis. The importance of systematization – a recurring topic in this chapter – was emphasized, as was the need to be open to alternative interpretations of the data. The chapter also stressed the importance of different verbal and non-verbal elements of content analysis. Each of these factors can shape and, hopefully, improve the content analysis you undertake – be it the classic content analysis highlighted in more detail above or some other approach to analysis.

In this chapter we also considered the different levels at which data analysis can occur. Building off previous work (Cyr 2016), we highlighted the relationship between the purpose of the focus group for the research project, the goals of the focus group data, and the level of data (individual, group, or interactive) at which you should focus your analysis. The amount of data that focus groups produce can be overwhelming. Having a sense of where to train your analytical eye can help you in this endeavor.

The chapter concluded with some tips on how to present your data, both in the more restricted space of the article-length format and in a less constrained medium, such as a book or a stand-alone report. In each section above, we emphasized that the research question, and the general goals of the overall project, should largely drive the choices you make as you analyze and present your data. Indeed, this point has been a running theme, not only in this chapter, but throughout the entire book.

Exercises

5.1. Choose a focus group-based project from the QDR, https://qdr.syr.edu/ (last accessed July 24, 2018). Download a transcript from the project. How would you proceed to analyze the transcript at the individual level? The group level? The interactive level?

5.2. Please turn once more to the same transcript from the QDR (see Exercise 5.1). This time, read the description of the project carefully. Summarize, first, what the purpose of the focus groups are for the overall research project (see Table 5.4 for examples). Then, describe what the objectives of the focus group data were. Does the proposed objective of the focus group data make sense given the purpose of the focus group in the larger project? Why or why not? Finally, given what you know about the purpose of the focus group and the data objectives, at which level(s) of analysis would you recommend the researcher focus her analytical attention? Why?

5.3. Continuing to rely on the same transcript from QDR (see Exercises 5.1 and 5.2), develop a set of instructions regarding how, exactly, you would analyze the content therein. What recommendations do you have for coding/classifying data? Are there any particular factors (e.g., frequency, extensiveness, context, time spent on a particular question) that you would want to take into account? What non-verbal cues, if any, should one look out for? (On this last question, you might need to be creative. If non-verbal signals are not included in the transcript, imagine what kinds of signals one might be on the look out for.) Once you have finished with the instructions, re-read what you have written. Imagine that you are forced to walk away from the project and not return to it for twelve months. Is what you have written sufficient to continue with the analysis? If not, what more would you add?

6 Conclusion

Throughout the pages of this book, I have sought to teach you about focus groups and to provide several important tips on how to carry them out from start to finish. Along the way, I hope you have learned a lot about the data collection method, including its practicalities, its challenges, and its rewards. In this brief conclusion, I intend to highlight the recurring themes that underpinned much of the book's content. These represent, to me, the most important things to keep in mind as you begin your own journey into focus group-based work.

First, I have emphasized the importance of the research question for shaping your approach to the data collection method. The research question should help define: your focus group goals, the purpose behind using focus groups, the information you hope to glean – basically everything focus group-related! On this point, focus groups are no different from any other data collection method. Still, we saw in Chapter 2 that focus groups are particularly useful for certain kinds of questions. For example, it makes sense to incorporate focus groups into your research design when you wish to understand group processes; when the topic is sensitive or taboo in nature and/or associated with vulnerable groups; and when key concepts under investigation need contextualization.

Focus groups are also useful when little is known about the question generally. We highlighted in Chapter 1 the emic nature of the data generated. In a focus group setting, the researcher will tend to ask open-ended questions that foster discussion. Because the participants do a lot of the conversational heavy lifting, focus groups are an excellent forum for exploring less known topics. The data they generate can therefore be useful for developing new hypotheses. They can also help define additional research questions.

We have also seen where they may *not* be appropriate. If your research question is oriented exclusively toward individual-level responses, for example, then the social setting of the focus group may confound your data collection process. Focus groups are inherently social in form. This is one of the method's strengths – a point we have underscored throughout much of the text. Still, given its social form, it can be difficult to isolate individual reactions from the group dynamic in which they are expressed. (Examining how individuals speak in a group setting is, however, another story – or, better said, another research question! One that focus groups can help you assess. See Table 2.1.)

Second, focus groups are highly versatile. They have multiple purposes and can be used for multiple projects. We highlighted, for example, the different levels of analysis at which data can be produced. Focus groups generate data at the individual, group, and interactive levels of analysis. In Chapter 5 we learned that there is a strong affinity between the purpose of focus groups for a research design and the level of analysis that might help us best achieve that purpose. This relationship has multiple implications for how we carry out focus groups.

For example, if a researcher is using focus groups to pre-test, contextualize, and/or refine certain questions on a survey, then she will likely focus her analytical attention on the group level of analysis. At the group level, conclusions are drawn regarding what kinds of meaning people assign to different words, phrases, or ideas. In understanding this affinity between the use of focus groups as pre-tests and the group level of analysis, the researcher also has some guidance in terms of how to present her overall findings. This is especially important in publication mediums that are restricted in terms of space.

Third, we have highlighted some of the (not insignificant) challenges that come with doing focus group-based work. For example, Chapters 3 and 4 highlighted the human factor as a potential source of difficulty. Certain participants can exhibit personality traits – being, for example, overly dominant or overly timid – that can affect the kind of data produced. The moderator must have the tools to restrain the prominent voices and draw out the quiet ones without disrupting the flow of the conversation. Overall, we saw that the moderator is a crucial element in executing a successful set of focus groups. She must facilitate the discussion without controlling it. She must probe in certain moments while sitting back to simply listen in others. Taking the time to instruct the moderator will be time well spent as you prepare to undertake focus groups. This might mean, as we saw in Chapter 3, paying special attention to the questions that are of particular importance; explaining when and where it might be useful to interject; and identifying the words and phrases she should avoid mentioning so as not to lead the group

An additional challenge consists in developing an effective question protocol. Chapter 3 emphasized that the questions that are asked – for example, whether they are open or closed in structure, the format they take, how varied they are – help to shape the data generated. As with training the moderator, the researcher will want to invest considerable time and energy in developing a question protocol. Generally speaking, questions should address the main points of interest, keep the participants engaged, and respect the time limits of the overall focus group.

Certainly, none of the challenges that can emerge during focus groups is insurmountable. Still, when they arise, you will want to address them quickly and effectively. Chapters 3 and 4 provide tips to help resolve those that may emerge. Overall, how your focus groups look in practice will likely diverge from the wish list you initially developed (see Table 3.1). This is okay, and it is to be expected.

Indeed, in acknowledging the challenges that can emerge with focus group-based work, I do not mean to dissuade you from utilizing focus groups in your research – far from it! Instead, I hope to have prepared you for some of the setbacks that will inevitably occur as you begin to collect data. Focus groups are not necessarily efficient, easy, or even cost-free. They are also not "soft," nor do they lack rigor. Indeed, we emphasized the importance of systematization at several steps throughout the data collection process. We saw in Chapter 3, for example, that practitioners should write down the decisions they make, and the logic underpinning those decisions, regarding how to prepare the moderator for the focus groups. Chapter 5 emphasized the importance of systematizing the data analysis, particularly in terms of how the data generated are coded and classified.

In sum, practitioners should strive to keep careful track of the choices made, the hurdles encountered, and the methods used to overcome those hurdles. In so doing, they will have a better sense of the ins and outs of the project overall. They will learn to expect, and therefore prevent, certain challenges in the future. And they will acquire the experience (based in no small part on their own institutional memory of past projects) to make each new focus group-based project increasingly manageable and beneficial.

Allow me to conclude by emphasizing one last thing. Focus groups can offer so much when it comes to understanding the world around us. They are also incredibly interesting, often illuminating, and really fun to undertake. Social scientists dedicate their lives to learning about how humans think, feel, interrelate, and act. These are big, important questions. They often involve multi-stage, multi-method responses. That we can be engaged, intrigued, and even delighted as we collect our data is no small thing, wouldn't you agree?

Appendix 1

Sample Question Protocol, with Instructions for the Moderator (*instructions are italicized*)

This protocol, which has been modified and simplified for instructional purposes from Cyr (2017b), was used for focus groups that addressed citizen perceptions of different "collapsed" political parties in Venezuela, Peru, and Bolivia. The questions here are contextualized for the country of Venezuela.

General Instructions to the Moderator

1. *Do not mention any party leader before s/he is first mentioned by someone in the group.*
2. *Do not use any descriptor or adjective about the political party in question unless someone uses the term first.*
3. *Ask participants to elaborate on their response if you feel it is unclear.*
4. *If participants veer away from the question at hand, remember to gently bring them back to the specific topic of the question. If, upon this gentle nudge, they still veer away from the question, then allow them to speak briefly before moving onto the next question.)*

Question Protocol

1. (Opening question): As I mentioned earlier, we hope to learn a bit about your impressions of different political parties in the country. Before we jump into the questions, however, I'd like each of you to tell us a bit about yourself. Please tell us your first name. Then, give us a sense of how interested you are in politics. Would you say that you spend a lot of time (maybe even daily!), some time, or not very much time thinking about politics?
2. (Introductory question): Now that we know each other, I want to start off with a bit of a memory exercise. Specifically, I'd like to ask you all to think back to the late 1990s. As you probably recall, in 1998, Hugo Chávez was elected to office in a fairly momentous election. Does everyone remember this election? (*The*

expectation here is that everyone will remember the election, since it totally upended the political status quo and dramatically changed democracy in the country. Still, if anyone looks confused or unsure, ask the group to talk about the importance of this election as a way to get them talking about this period.) Now I'd like you to think about the political parties that used to dominate Venezuelan politics. I would like each of you to think back to the late 1990s and tell us a story about *Acción Democrática* (AD) that you remember from that time. It can be an anecdote about a particular party member or a general impression that you recall having about the party at the time. You can tell me anything from that period that you can recall about AD. I'll give you a minute or two to think about it. Then we will go around the table, and I'll ask each of you to tell your story.

(Note that this is the last question where you specifically call on each person to give an answer. After this, allow individuals to volunteer their responses and let participants respond to each other as they wish.

If the participants seem cautious or timid regarding how to answer this question, you can offer a few ideas. Perhaps they recall something that appeared on the news at the time – a story about AD or about an AD politician. Perhaps they recall a conversation with a family member or neighbor.)

3. Now that we have recalled a couple of stories from that time, I'd like to know what you remember thinking about AD, that is, what your opinion of the party was. In other words, at that time in the late 1990s, how would you have described AD? Please use the paper and pen in front of you to write down three words or phrases that would have come to mind . . . three words or phrases that best describe what the party meant to you at that time. These can be anything. Once you've written them down, we'll go around the table, and everyone can tell us what they wrote.

(For this question, you might have to ask them to elaborate. Why did they choose the words or phrases that they did?

Where two individuals have contradictory opinions, ask the group to ponder this. Why might this party provoke such different reactions?

If there is a lot of agreement, by contrast, you can also mention this to the group and ask them why they think there is such a consensus about the party.)

4. What about COPEI? I'm curious to know how you all would have described the party at that time. What words or phrases would you use to describe the party? As with AD, please write down up to three words or phrases that you might have used about the party in the late 1990s.
5. I'm now going to show you a series of images. I'll ask you to identify the images, if you can, and to share your reactions to these images. What does the image mean to you? What do you think it means for Venezuela?

Remember that we don't have to agree about these images and what they mean to us.

(For each party, please first show a picture of the political party's logo, then a picture of the political party's founder, and, finally, a picture of the most recent president from the party.)

6. (Ranking exercise): As you all know, politics has changed since Hugo Chávez was elected. For one thing, we have a new constitution! Also, new political parties are competing, and new politicians are being elected into office. Let's talk about these changes. What has changed positively since Chávez was elected in 1998? To answer this question, I'd like us to come up with a list of the three most positive changes that the country has undergone.

(The idea here is to see if there is consensus about these changes. Allow them to discuss and debate this point.)

7. What about negative changes? Can you identify three or more negative changes that the country's political system has undergone?

(Here the goal is not to rank, although they can if they wish to.)

8. Now I'd like us all to think about AD today. *(There might be some surprise to this question, since the party is not particularly visible in politics today.)* I'd like you to think about what you know or have seen about AD more recently, let's say over the last five years. What do you think about AD today? Has your attitude toward the party changed?

8a. Ask the same question about COPEI.

9. I have one last question for you all. As you know, neither AD nor COPEI has been very successful at fielding presidential candidates over the last ten years. Why do you think this is? Why do you think that Venezuelans stopped voting for these parties? In your opinion, what would each party have to do differently so that people would begin voting for it again? Let's begin first with AD and then consider COPEI.

10. (Final, reflective question): Is there anything else you'd like to mention about either AD or COPEI? Something you'd like to add that hasn't already been mentioned?

Thank you very much for your time! Remember that you can contact Jennifer Cyr if you have any questions or comments about our conversation today. Feel free to speak with her now or to take her business card to follow up later.

Appendix 2

Additional Analytical Tools Available to the Focus Group Researcher

There are multiple qualitative data analysis software options available to a researcher – so many that it is difficult to include them all, even in an appendix, and have it be user friendly. In what follows, I provide a brief summary of five of the most widely used qualitative data analysis programs (see, e.g., Silver and Lewins 2014; Anderson-Gough et al. 2017).[1]

Note that all five programs will help a researcher undertake coding and text mining. They offer mapping and hyperlinking tools, which help integrate different texts, and the memo-writing tools that are necessary for framework analysis (Silver and Lewins 2014). Note, too, that the software manufacturers regularly issue updates on certain, less stable parameters (e.g., their cost, platform, help and support packages, etc.). Providing a comparison on these counts, therefore, would quickly become out-of-date – possibly even before this final text is published. Given this, I have decided simply to provide a summary of each software option. For the latest information on the specific features attached to each software package, see https://study.sagepub.com/using-software-in-qualitative-research (last accessed July 25, 2018) or the company websites for each program.

While these are the most common software packages, I make no judgment regarding how useful these packages are vis-à-vis others that are available (see footnote 1). The summaries are based on those provided by Silver and Lewins (2014, Chapter 3), who in turn rely in part on company descriptions of each package. The descriptions are intended to highlight some of the unique features of each program. For further information on any individual package, please consult the company's website.

One final note. Chapter 5 provides instructions on how to undertake analysis without the help of software. Whether or not a researcher uses software to analyze the content of focus group conversations, it is important that she know the basics of the process through which analysis occurs. Still, there are certain advantages to

[1] Note that these five software programs are just some of the myriad options available to a researcher, each with its own set of strengths and weaknesses. Additional programs include, but certainly are not limited to, the following: Dedoose, f4analyse, Kwalitan, Leximancer, Quirkos, Raven's Eye, Saturate, Transana, webQDA, and Weft QDA.

computer-assisted qualitative data analysis (CAQDAS). For one, you can "play" with the data in ways that are more difficult by hand. You can rely on the program to help develop an organizing system for the focus group content. This can be especially useful if you have a lot of transcriptions to analyze. CAQDAS also allows you to create and share large datasets, which can facilitate group projects and allows for secondary analysis of conversations.

Below you will find brief summaries of ATLAS.ti, HyperRESEARCH, MAXQDA, NVivo, and QDA Miner.

ATLAS.ti. This package involves moving back and forth between data functions, including segmenting, coding, and memoing, and more conceptual functions, such as theory-building. Like many software packages, it supports code-based approaches to data analysis. It also, however, allows the researcher to prioritize the tracking of non-linear and non-thematic associations, including forms of narrative, discourse, and linguistic analysis. Its quotation structure enables the researcher to build different data segments, code them, and link them in such a way as to represent rhetoric structure or track a story/process. ATLAS.ti allows the researcher to link different types of media. Its margin display facilitates data manipulation. Additionally, the researcher can display up to four documents on the screen simultaneously. The package has a super-code function, which enables the researcher to treat queries like codes. Finally, the package provides a mobile app, which can be used as a field recorder.

HyperRESEARCH. Unlike the other packages summarized here, HyperRESEARCH supports a case-based (rather than code-based) structure for comparative analysis. A case is defined by the researcher and consists of any grouping that can be compared, for example, individual study subjects, organizations, different groups of individuals, a dimension of analysis, or entire focus groups. The software can link multiple data sources to multiple cases. A Report Builder feature allows multiple ways to display findings. A Theory Builder feature allows for the identification of themes in the data. The package works on Mac and Windows and files can be easily transferred between each platform.

MAXQDA. This software package supports the analysis of qualitative and mixed data through a variety of approaches, including grounded theory, thematic analysis, discourse analysis, phenomenology, ethnography, and content analysis. It is a code-based system and allows the researcher to work with a framework of categories that are developed iteratively as analysis unfolds. Its visualizations, and in particular its versatile and extensive use of color to identify codes, are unique in their sophistication and flexibility. The package offers multiple visual tools and functions that support mixed-methods analysis. MAXMaps allows for the production of different concept maps. Diagrams, including Codeline, Document Portrait, and Text Comparison Chart, offer unique cross-sectional perspectives of text. In addition to qualitative data, the software can directly import and auto-process survey data from spreadsheet applications.

NVivo. A code-based system, NVivo is particularly suited for supporting structured qualitative data and has added features that allow for the incorporation of materials from other applications. For example, NCapture allows researchers to work with social media data, such as Facebook and Twitter. Additional features interact with note-taking tools and reference packages, such as Zotero and Endnote. The program also allows you to directly import from Survey Monkey. The program features the use of nodes, which organize information and/or sources. Thematic nodes enable coding. NVivo also allows the researcher to create relationship nodes. With these, one can express relationships between concepts or respondents and provide a space where evidence for those relationships can be coded. These connections (and others) can then be illustrated graphically using the modeling tool. Finally, NVivo provides an Externals folder, where proxy files can be created to represent data that cannot be imported.

QDA Miner. This package allows for the storage of qualitative and quantitative data within one file. It is unique in the kinds of mixed-methods analytic support it provides. QDA Miner enables the researcher to consider qualitative data from multiple epistemological perspectives. It also integrates statistical and visualization tools, including clustering, multidimensional scaling, and sequence analysis, and allows the researcher to undertake basic statistical tests. Two add-on modules, WordStat and Simstat, allow the researcher to carry out more sophisticated text mining and statistical analysis. The package allows the researcher to create an entire project file by selecting multiple files from a folder or data from a spreadsheet. It also provides a series of pattern-matching tools that allow coding to be as consistent as possible across data sources. Report Manager allows the researcher to organize and store, for example, data analysis, tables, graphs, and quotes in one location, which facilitates the writing process.

Works Cited

Abdelal, Rawi, Yoshiko M. Herrera, Alastair Iain Johnston, and Rose McDermott, eds. 2009. In *Measuring Identity: A Guide for Social Scientists*. Cambridge: Cambridge University Press.

Adcock, Robert and David Collier. 2001. "Measurement Validity: A Shared Standard for Qualitative and Quantitative Research." *American Political Science Review* 95 (3):529–546.

Agar, Michael and James MacDonald. 1995. "Focus Groups and Ethnography." *Human Organization* 54 (1): 78–86.

Ahmed, Ariel, and Rudra Sil. 2012. "When Multi-Method Research Subverts Methodological Pluralism – or, Why We Still Need Single-Method Research." *Perspectives on Politics* 10(4): 935–953.

Albrecht, Terrance L., Gerianne M. Johnson, and Joseph B. Walther. 1993. "Understanding Communication Processes in Focus Groups." In *Successful Focus Groups: Advancing the State of the Art*. David L. Morgan, ed., Newbury Park, CA: Sage Publications.

Allport, Floyd H. 1920. "The Influence of the Group upon Association and Thought." *Journal of Experimental Psychology* 3: 159–182.

1924. *Social Psychology*. Boston, MA: Houghton Mifflin.

Anderson-Gough, Fiona, Carla Edgley, and Nina Sharma. 2017. "Qualitative Data Management and Analysis Software." In *The Routledge Companion to Qualitative Accounting Research Methods*. Zahirul Hoque, Lee D. Parker, Mark Covaleski, and Kathryn Haynes, eds., New York: Routledge.

Andersson, Steffan and Paul M. Heywood. 2009. "The Politics of Perception: Use and Abuse of Transparency International's Approach to Measuring Corruption." *Political Studies* 57: 746–767.

Ayrton, Rachel. 2018. "The Micro-dynamics of Power and Performance in Focus Groups: An Example from Discussions on National Identity with the South Sudanese Diaspora in the UK." *Qualitative Research*. First published online February 14, 2018: 1–17.

Babbie, Earl R. 1998. *The Practice of Social Research*. Vol. 112. Belmont, CA: Wadsworth Publishing Company.

Barabas, Jason. 2004. "How Deliberation Affects Policy Opinions." *American Political Science Review* 98: 687–701.

Barbour, Rosaline. 2008. *Doing Focus Groups*.Thousand Oaks, CA: Sage.

Barbour, Rosaline and Jenny Kitzinger.1999. *Developing Focus Group Research*. London: Sage Publications.

Bloor, Michael, Jane Frankland, Michelle Thomas, and Kate Robson. 2001. *Focus Groups in Social Research*. London: Sage Publications.

Borkan, Jeffrey M., Mohammed Morad, and Shifra Shvarts. 2000. "Universal Health Care? The Views of Negev Bedouin Arabs on Health Services." *Health Policy and Planning* 15 (2): 207–216.

Bradbury-Jones, Caroline, Sally Sambrook, and Fiona Irvine. 2008. "Power and Empowerment in Nursing: a Fourth Theoretical Approach." *Journal of Advanced Nursing* 62 (2): 258–266.

Bratton, Michael and Beatrice Liatto-Katundu. 1994. "A Focus Group Assessment of Political Attitudes in Zambia." *African Affairs* 93: 535–563.

Calder, Bobby J. 1977. "Focus Groups and the Nature of Qualitative Marketing Research." *Journal of Marketing Research* XIV: 353–364.

Campbell, Donald T., and Julian C. Stanley. 1963. "Experimental and Quasi-experimental Designs for Research." In *Handbook of Research on Teaching.* N. L. Gage, ed., Chicago, IL: Rand McNally.

Carey, Martha A. 1994. "The Group Effect in Focus Groups: Planning, Implementing and Interpreting Focus Group Research." In *Critical Issues in Qualitative Research Methods.* J. M. Morse, ed., London: Sage.

Carey, Martha Ann and Mickey W. Smith. 1994. "Capturing the Group Effect in Focus Groups: A Special Concern in Analysis." *Qualitative Health Research* 4 (1): 123–127.

Caruso, Thomas E. 1976. "Moderators Focus on Groups: Session 7 Yields Hypotheses Covering Technology Trend, Professionalism, Training Techniques, Reports, etc." *Marketing News* 10 (10): 12–16.

Chadda, M. 2004. "India: Between Majesty and Modernity." In *The Struggle against Corruption: A Comparative Study.* R.A. Johnson, ed., New York: Palgrave Macmillan.

Chaiken, Shelly. 1980. "Heuristic Versus Systematic Information Processing and the Use of Source Versus Message Cues in Persuasion." *Journal of Personality and Social Psychology* 39: 752–766.

Chatterjee, Abhishek. 2013. "Ontology, Epistemology, and Multimethod Research in Political Science." *Philosophy of the Social Sciences* 43(1): 73–99.

Colucci, Erminia. 2007. "'Focus Groups Can be Fun': The Use of Activity-Oriented Questions in Focus Group Discussions." *Qualitative Health Research* 17 (10): 1422–1433.

Copsey, Nathaniel. 2008. "Focus Groups and the Political Scientist." European Research Working Paper, Series No. 22. Edgbaston, UK: The University of Birmingham.

Cyr, Jennifer. 2016. "The Pitfalls and Promise of Focus Groups as a Data Collection Method." *Sociological Methods and Research 45 (2): 231-259.*

2017a. *The Fates of Political Parties: Institutional Crisis, Continuity, and Change in Latin America*. Cambridge: Cambridge University Press.

2017b. "The Unique Utility of Focus Groups for Mixed-Methods Research." *PS: Political Science and Politics 50 (4): 1038–1041.*

Cyr, Jennifer and Carlos Meléndez. 2017. "Anti-Identities in Latin America: *Chavismo, Fujimorismo*, and *Uribismo* in Comparative Perspective." Paper prepared for the 74th Annual Midwest Political Science Association Conference. Chicago, IL: April 7–10, 2016.

Denzin, N. 2006. *Sociological Methods: A Sourcebook*. 5th edition. Chicago, IL: Aldine Transaction.

DiMaggio, Paul and Filiz Garip. 2011. "How Network Externalities Can Exacerbate Intergroup Inequality." *American Journal of Sociology* 116: 1887–1933.

Doody, Owen, Eamonn Slevin, and Laurence Taggart. 2013. "Focus Group Interviews. Part 3: Analysis." *British Journal of Nursing* 22 (5): 266–269.

Duggleby, Wendy. 2005. "What about Focus Group Interaction Data?" *Qualitative Health Research* 15 (6): 832–840.

Ehrlich, Howard J. 1973. *The Social Psychology of Prejudice; A Systematic Theoretical Review and Propositional Inventory of the American Social Psychological Study of Prejudice*. New York: Wiley.

Farnsworth, John and Bronwyn Boon. 2010. "Analysing Group Dynamics Within the Focus Group." *Qualitative Research* 10: 605–624.

Farquhar, Claire and Rita Das. 1999. "Are Focus Groups Suitable for 'Sensitive' Topics?" In *Developing Focus Group Research*. Rosaline Barbour and Jenny Kitzinger, eds., London: Sage.

Fern, Edward F. 1982. "The Use of Focus Groups for Idea Generation: The Effects of Group Size, Acquaintanceship, and Moderator on Response Quantity and Quality." *Journal of Marketing Research* 19: 1–13.

2001. *Advanced Focus Group Research*. London: Sage Publications.

Finch, Helen, and Jane Lewis. 2003. "Focus Groups." In *Qualitative Research Practice: A Guide for Social Science Students and Researchers*. Jane Ritchie and Jane Lewis, eds., London: Sage Publications.

Finch, Helen, Jane Lewis, and Caroline Turley. 2014. "Focus Groups." In *Qualitative Research Practice: A Guide for Social Science Students and Researchers*. Jane Ritchie, Jane Lewis, Carol McNaughton Nicholls, and Rachel Ormston, eds., London: Sage Publications.

Flick, Uwe. 2009. *An Introduction to Qualitative Research*. 4th edition. London: Sage Publications.

Frank, Mark G., and Thomas Gilovich. 1988. "The Dark Side of Self- and Social Perception: Black Uniforms and Aggression in Professional Sports." *Journal of Personality and Social Psychology* 54 (1): 74–85.

Fuller, Theodore, John Edwards, Sairudee Vorakithphokatorn, and Santhat Sermsri. 1993. "Using Focus Groups to Adapt Survey Instruments to New Populations." In *Successful Focus Groups: Advancing the State of the Art*. D. Morgan, ed., Newbury Park, CA: Sage.

Gaiser, Ted J. 2008. "Online Focus Groups." In *The Sage Handbook of Online Research Methods*. N. G. Fielding, R. M. Lee, and G. Blank, eds., London: Sage Publications.

Gamson, William A. 1992. *Talking Politics*. Cambridge: Cambridge University Press.

Garvía, Roberto. 2007. "Syndication, Institutionalization, and Lottery Play." *American Journal of Sociology* 113: 603–652.

Gerber, Alan and Neil Malhotra. 2008. "Do Statistical Reporting Standards Affect What Is Published? Publication Bias in Two Leading Political Science Journals." *Quarterly Journal of Political Science* 3: 313–326.

Gibson, James L. 2004. "Does Truth Lead to Reconciliation? Testing the Causal Assumptions of the South African Truth and Reconciliation Process." *American Journal of Political Science* 48: 201–217.

Goertz, Gary, and James Mahoney. 2012. *A Tale of Two Cultures: Qualitative and Quantitative Research in the Social Sciences.* Princeton, NJ: Princeton University Press.

Gothberg, June, Patricia Reeves, Linda Thurston, Brooks Applegate, Paula Kohler, and Lori Peterson. 2013. "Is the Medium Really the Message? A Comparison of Face-to-Face, Telephone, and Internet Focus Group Venues." *Journal of Ethnographic and Qualitative Research* 7 (3): 108–127.

Green, Donald P., Bradley Palmquist, and Eric Schickler. 2002. *Partisan Hearts and Minds: Political Parties and the Social Identities of Voters.* New Haven, CT: Yale University Press.

Hennink, Monique M. 2007. *International Focus Group Research: A Handbook for the Health and Social Sciences.* Cambridge: Cambridge University Press.

2010. "Emergent Issues in International Focus Group Discussions." In *Handbook of Emergent Methods.* Sharlene Nagy Hesse-Biber and Patricia Leavy, eds., New York: Guilford Press.

Hesse-Biber, Sharlene Nagy, and Patricia Leavy. 2010. *The Practice of Qualitative Research.* Thousand Oaks, CA: Sage.

Hollander, Jocelyn A. 2004. "The Social Contexts of Focus Groups." *Journal of Contemporary Ethnography* 33: 602–637.

Humphreys, Macartan, and Alan M. Jacobs. 2015. Mixing Methods: A Bayesian Approach. *American Political Science Review* 109(4): 653–673.

Hunleth, Jean. 2011. "Beyond on or with: Questioning Power Dynamics and Knowledge Production in 'Child-Oriented' Research Methodology." *Childhood* 18 (1): 81–93.

Hunter, Wendy, and Natasha Borges Sugiyama. 2014. "Transforming Subjects into Citizens: Insights from Brazil's Bolsa Família." *Perspectives on Politics* 12(4): 829–845.

Jakobsen, Hilde. 2012. "Focus Groups and Methodological Rigour outside the Minority World: Making the Method Work to Its Strengths in Tanzania." *Qualitative Research* 12 (2): 111–130.

Kidd, Pamela S., and Mark B. Parshall. 2000. "Getting the Focus and the Group: Enhancing Analytical Rigor in Focus Group Research." *Qualitative Health Research* 10 (3): 293–308.

Kitzinger, Jenny. 1994. "The Methodology of Focus Groups: The Importance of Interaction between Research Participants." *Sociology of Health and Illness* 16 (1): 103–121.

1995. "The Methodology of Focus Groups: The Importance of Interaction between Research Participants." *Sociology of Health and Illness* 16: 103–121.

2004. "The Grit in the Oyster: Analysing Phrases, Anecdotes, Analogies, Associations and Silences in Focus Groups." *Bulletin de Psychologie* 57: 299–308.

2005. "Focus Group Research: Using Group Dynamics to Explore Perceptions, Experience and Understandings." In *Qualitative Research in Health Care.* Immy Holloway, ed., Maidenhead: Open University Press.

Kitzinger, Jenny, and Rosaline Barbour 1999. *Developing Focus Group Research.* London: Sage Publications.

Kosny, Agnieszka. 2003. "Joint Stories and Layered Tales: Support, Contradiction and Meaning Construction in Focus Group Research." *The Qualitative Report* 8: 539–548. Available at https://nsuworks.nova.edu/tqr/vol8/iss4/2/ (last accessed August 10, 2018).

Kottak, C. P., 1996, *Mirror for Humanity.* New York: McGraw-Hill.

Krippendorf, Klaus. 2004. *Content Analysis: An Introduction to its Methodology.* 2nd edition. Thousand Oaks, CA: Sage.

Kroll, Thilo, Rosaline Barbour, and Jennifer Harris. 2007. "Using Focus Groups in Disability Research." *Qualitative Health Research* 17 (5): 690–698.

Krosnick, Jon A. 1991. "Response Strategies for Coping with the Cognitive Demands of Attitude Measures in Surveys." *Applied Cognitive Psychology* 5: 213–236.

Krosnick, Jon A., Sowmya Narayan, and Wendy R. Smith. 1996. "Satisficing in Surveys: Initial Evidence." *New Directions for Evaluation* 70: 29–44.

Krueger, Richard A. 1994. *Focus Groups: A Practical Guide for Applied Research.* Thousand Oaks, CA: Sage.

1998a. "Developing Questions for Focus Groups." In *Focus Group Kit* (Vol. 3), David Morgan, Richard A. Krueger, and J. A. King, eds., Thousand Oaks, CA: Sage.

1998b. "Analyzing and Reporting Focus Group Results." In *Focus Group Kit* (Vol. 3), David Morgan, Richard A. Krueger, and J. A. King, eds., Thousand Oaks, CA: Sage.

Krueger, Richard A. and M. A. Casey. 1994. *Focus Groups: A Practical Guide for Applied Research.* Thousand Oaks, CA: Sage.

2000. *Focus Groups: A Practical Guide for Applied Research.* 3rd edition. Thousand Oaks, CA: Sage Publications.

2015. "Focus Group Interviewing Research Methods: Notes." https://richardakrueger.com/focus-group-interviewing/ (last accessed, May 15, 2017).

Krueger, Richard A., Mary Anne Casey, Jonathan Donner, Stuart Kirsch, and Jonathan Maack. 2001. "Social Analysis, Selected Tools and Techniques." Paper Number 36. World Bank: http://web.worldbank.org/archive/website01028/WEB/IMAGES/SDP_36.PDF#page=10 (last accessed March 31, 2017).

Krysan, Maria, Mick P. Couper, Reynolds Farley, and Tyrone A. Forman. 2009. "Does Race Matter in Neighborhood Preferences? Results from a Video Experiment." *American Journal of Sociology* 115: 527–559.

Kvale, Steinar. 2006. "Dominance through Interviews and Dialogues." *Qualitative Inquiry* 12 (3): 480–500.

Lambert, Sylvie D., and Carmen G. Loiselle. 2008. "Combining Individual Interviews and Focus Groups to Enhance Data Richness." *Journal of Advanced Nursing* 62 (2): 228–237.

Lett, J. 1990. "Emics and Etics: Notes on the Epistemology of Anthropology." In *Emics and Etics: The Insider/Outsider Debate.* Frontiers of Anthropology, Vol. 7., T. N. Headland, K. L. Pike, and M. Harris, eds., Newbury Park, CA: Sage Publications.

Leyens, J. P. H., V. Y. Yzerbyt, and G. Schadron. 1994. *Stereotypes and Social Cognition.* London: Sage.

Lezuan, Javier. 2007. "A Market of Opinions: The Political Epistemology of Focus Groups." *The Sociological Review* 55: 130–151.

Liamputtong, Pranee. 2011. *Focus Group Methodology: Principles and Practice.* London: Sage Publications, Ltd.

Lieberman, Evan S. 2005. "Nested Analysis as a Mixed-Method Strategy for Comparative Research." *American Political Science Review* 99 (3): 435–452.

Lupu, Noam. 2013. "Party Brands and Partisanship: Theory with Evidence from a Survey Experiment in Argentina." *American Journal of Political Science* 57 (January): 49–64.

Madriz, Esther. 1997. *Nothing Bad Happens to Good Girls: Fear of Crime in Women's Lives.* Los Angeles, *CA:* University of California Press.

Marková, Ivana. 2007. *Dialogue in Focus Groups: Exploring Socially Shared Knowledge* London: Equinox.

McDonald, William J. 1993. "Focus Group Research Dynamics and Reporting: An Examination of Research Objectives and Moderator Influences." *Journal of the Academy of Marketing Science* 21 (2): 161–168.

McGrath, Joseph E. 1982. "Dilemmatics: The Study of Research Choices and Dilemmas." In *Judgment Calls in Research.* Joseph E. McGrath, Joanne Martin, and Richard A. Kulka, eds., Beverly Hills, CA: Sage.

Merton, Robert K. 1987. "The Focussed Interview and Focus Groups: Continuities and Discontinuities." *The Public Opinion Quarterly* 51(4): 550–566.

Merton, Robert K., and Patricia L. Kendall. 1946. "The Focused Interview." *American Journal of Sociology* 51(6): 541–557.

Merton, Robert K., Marjorie Fiske, and Patricia Kendall. 1956. *The Focused Interview; A Manual of Problems and Procedures.* New York: Free Press.

Moore, Mignon R. 2008. "Gendered Power Relations among Women: A Study of Household Decision Making in Black, Lesbian Stepfamilies." *American Sociological Review* 73: 335–356.

Morgan, David. 1988. *Focus Groups as Qualitative Research.* Sage Publications series on Qualitative Research Methods, Vol. 16. Thousand Oaks, CA: Sage.

ed. 1993. *Successful Focus Groups: Advancing the State of the Art.* Newbury Park, CA: Sage Publications.

1995. "Why Things (Sometimes) Go Wrong in Focus Groups." *Qualitative Health Research* 5(4): 516–523.

1996. "Focus Groups." *Annual Review of Sociology* 22 (1): 129–152.

1997. *Focus Groups as Qualitative Research.* Thousand Oaks, CA: Sage Publications.

Morgan, David L. and Richard Krueger. 1993. "When to Use Focus Groups and Why." In *Successful Focus Groups: Advancing the State of the Art.* David Morgan, ed., Newbury Park, CA: Sage.

Morrison-Beedy, Dianne, Denise Côté-Arsenault, and Nancy Fischbeck Feinstein. 2001. "Maximizing Results with Focus Groups: Moderator and Analysis Issues." *Applied Nursing Research* 14 (1): 48–53.

Munday, Jennie. 2006. "Identity in Focus: The Use of Focus Groups to Study the Construction of Collective Identity." *Sociology* 40: 89–105.

Myers, David. 2008. *Matters of Public Opinion: Talking about Public Issues.* New York: Cambridge University Press.

Nickerson, David W. 2007. "Quality Is Job One: Professional and Volunteer Voter Mobilization Calls." *American Journal of Political Science* 51: 269–282.

O'Brien, K. 1993a. Improving Survey Questionnaires through Focus Groups." In *Successful Focus Groups: Advancing the State of the Art.* David Morgan, ed., Newbury Park, CA: Sage Publications.

1993b. "Using Focus Groups to Develop Health Surveys: An Example from Research on Social Relationships and AIDS-Preventive Behavior." *Health Education Quarterly* 20 (3): 361–372.

Onwuegbuzie, Anthony J., Wendy B. Dickinson, Nancy L. Leech, and Annmarie G. Zoran. 2009. "A Qualitative Framework for Collecting and Analyzing Data in Focus Group Research." *International Journal of Qualitative Methods* 8 (3): 1–21.

Palmer, Michelle, Michael Larkin, Richard de Visser and Grainne Fadden. 2010. "Developing an Interpretative Phenomenological Approach to Focus Group Data." *Qualitative Research in Psychology* 7 (2): 99–121.

Paluck, Elizabeth Levy. 2010. "The Promising Integration of Qualitative Methods and Field Experiments." *The Annals of the American Academy of Political and Social Science* 628: 59–71.

Paluck, Elizabeth Levy, and Donald P. Green. 2009. "Deference, Dissent, and Dispute Resolution: An Experimental Intervention Using Mass Media to Change Norms and Behaviors in Rwanda." *American Political Science Review* 103(4): 622–644.

Posner, Daniel. 2005. *Institutions and Ethnic Politics in Africa.* Cambridge: Cambridge University Press.

Prabhakar, Rajiv. 2012. "What Do the Public Think of Taxation? Evidence from a Focus Group Study in England." *Journal of European Social Policy* 22: 77–89.

Puchta, Claudia and Jonathan Potter. 2002. "Manufacturing Individual Opinions: Market Research Focus Groups and the Discursive Psychology of Evaluation." *British Journal of Social Psychology* 41: 345–363.

2004. *Focus Group Practice.* Thousand Oaks, CA: Sage.

Renzetti, Claire and Raymond Lee. 1993. *Researching Sensitive Topics.* Newbury Park, CA: Sage Publications.

Ruthmann, S. A. 2008. “Whose Agency Matters? Negotiating Pedagogical Experiences and Creative Intent during Composing Experiences.” *Research Studies in Music Education* 30(1): 43–58.

Schindler, Robert M. 1992. “The Real Lesson of New Coke: The Value of Focus Groups for Predicting the Effects of Social Influence.” *Marketing Research: A Magazine of Management and Applications* 4: 22–27.

Schutt, Russell K. 2011. *Investigating the Social World: The Process and Practice of Research*. Thousand Oaks, CA: Sage Publications.

Seawright, Jason. 2016. *Multi-Method Social Science: Combining Qualitative and Quantitative Tools*. Cambridge: Cambridge University Press.

Short, Susan. 2006. “Focus group interviews.” In *A Handbook for Social Science Field Research: Essays and Bibliographic Sources on Research Design, Methodology, and Fieldwork*. Ellen Perecman and Sara R. Curran, eds., Thousand Oaks, CA: Sage Publications.

Silver, Christina, and Ann Lewins. 2014. *Using Software in Qualitative Research: A Step-by-step Guide*, 2nd edition. London: Sage Publications.

Sim, Julius. 1998. “Collecting and Analysing Qualitative Data: Issues Raised by the Focus Group.” *Journal of Advanced Nursing* 28 (2): 345–352.

Smith, Joanna M., S. John Sullivan, and G. David Baxter. 2009. “Telephone Focus Groups in Physiotherapy Research: Potential Uses and Recommendations.” *Physiotherapy Theory and Practice* 25 (4): 241–256.

Smithson, Janet. 2000. “Using and Analysing Focus Groups: Limitations and Possibilities.” *International Journal of Social Research Methodology* 3: 103–119.

Stark, Laura. 2011. *Behind Closed Doors: IRBs and the Making of Ethical Research*. Chicago, IL: University of Chicago Press.

Stevens, Patricia E. 1996. “Focus groups: Collecting aggregate-level data to understand community health phenomena.” *Public Health Nursing* 13 (3): 170–176.

Stewart, David W. and Prem N. Shamdasani.1990. *Focus Groups: Theory and Practice*. Thousand Oaks, CA: Sage.

Stewart, David W., Prem N. Shamdasani, and Dennis W. Rook. 2007. *Focus Groups: Theory and Practice*. 2nd edition. Thousand Oaks, CA: Sage Publications.

2009. “Group Depth Interviews: Focus Group Research.” In *The Sage Handbook of Applied Social Research Methods*. L. Bickman and D. J. Rog, eds, Los Angeles, CA: Sage.

Stoddart, Mark C. J. 2004. “Generalizability and Qualitative Research in a Postmodern World.” *Graduate Journal of Social Science* 1 (2): 303–317.

Tarrow, Sidney. 1995. “Bridging the Quantitative-Qualitative Divide in Political Science.” *American Political Science Review* 89 (2): 471–474.

Tajfel, Henri. 1970. “Experiments in Intergroup Discrimination.” *Scientific American* 223 (5): 96–103.

Tajfel, Henri, Michael G. Billig, Robert P. Bundy, and Claude Flament. 1971. “Social Categorization and Intergroup Behaviour.” *European Journal of Social Psychology* 1 (2): 149–178.

Tourangeau, Roger. 1984. "Cognitive Sciences and Survey Methods." In *Cognitive Aspects of Survey Methodology: Building a Bridge between Disciplines.* Thomas B. Jabine, Miron L. Straf, Judith M. Tanur, and Roger Tourangeau, eds., Washington, DC: National Academy Press.

Vicsek, Lilla. 2010. "Issues in the Analysis of Focus Groups: Generalisability, Quantifiability, Treatment of Context and Quotations." *The Qualitative Report* 15: 122–141.

Vissandjee, Bilkis, Shelly N. Abdool, and Sophie Dupéré. 2002. "Focus Groups in Rural Gujarat, India: A Modified Approach." *Qualitative Health Research* 12 (6): 826–843.

Wellings, Kaye, Patrick Branigan, and Kirsti Mitchell. 2000. "Discomfort, Discord and Discontinuity as Data: Using Focus Groups to Research Sensitive Topics." *Culture, Health and Sexuality* 2 (3): 255–267.

Wells, William D. 1979. "Group Interviewing." In *Focus Group Interviews: A Reader.* James B. Higginbotham and Keith K. Cox, eds., Chicago, IL: American Marketing Association.

Wilkins Winslow, Wendy, Gladys Honein, and Margaret Ann Elzubeir. 2002. "Seeking Emirati Women's Voices: The Use of Focus Groups with an Arab Population." *Qualitative Health Research* 12 (4): 566–575.

Wilkinson, Sue. 1999. "Focus Groups: A Feminist Method." *Psychology of Women Quarterly* 23 (2): 221–244.

2006. "Analyzing Interaction in Focus Groups." In *Talk and Interaction in Social Research Methods.* P. Drew, G. Raymond, and D. Weinberg, eds., London: Sage.

2016. "Analysing Focus Group Data." In *Qualitative Research.* David Silverman, ed., 4th edition. Thousand Oaks, CA: Sage.

Yanow, Dvora. 2015. *Constructing "race" and "ethnicity" in America: Category-Making in Public Policy and Administration.* New York: Routledge.

Index